THE ROOT OF THE MATTER

THE ROOT
of the
MATTER

*Boyhood Manhood
and God*

FATHER
ANTHONY ROSS

MAINSTREAM
PUBLISHING

All rights reserved
First published in Great Britain in 1989 by
MAINSTREAM PUBLISHING COMPANY (EDINBURGH) LTD
7 Albany Street
Edinburgh EH1 3UG

ISBN 1 85158 250 9 (cloth)

The publisher acknowledges the financial assistance of the Scottish Arts
Council in the production of this volume.

British Libray Catalogue in Publication Data
Ross, Anthony, *1917–*
    The root of the matter
    1. Scotland, Catholic Church. Ross, Anthony,
    1917–
    I. Title
    282'.092'4

ISBN 1–85158–250–9

Typeset in 11 on 12pt Imprint by C. R. Barber & Partners (Highlands)
Limited, Fort William, Scotland
Printed in Great Britain by Billings & Sons, Worcester

To Jessie and Donald Ross and Margaret Ross:

'love covers over all offences'
Proverbs, x. 12

ACKNOWLEDGEMENTS

Father Anthony would like to thank a number of friends for helping him with the initial preparation of this book, particularly Robert Sutherland, Charles Gruar Murray, James Claffey O.P. and Bill Jordan. He would like to pay particular tribute to Mrs Sheila Webb, whose devoted work on his secretarial needs for many years preserved so much material for it. He wants to thank Owen Dudley Edwards for helping to prepare it for publication. Together with the publishers he wishes also to thank Mrs T. S. Eliot and Messrs Faber & Faber for permission to quote from T. S. Eliot's 'The Love Song of J. Alfred Prufrock' and 'Sweeney Among the Nightingales'.

PART ONE

I

The house stood between forest and moor, high above the river plain, in a clearing of a few acres. From a point not far from where the road entered the wood there was a clear view on good days over the village of Beauly, and down the Beauly Firth to a point on the south side of the Black Isle opposite Inverness. On the June night on which I was born a gale stormed the trees and my grandmother prayed loudly and anxiously, being afraid that the lime tree at the east end of the house would fall and kill mother and child. She was great at anticipating the worst, and when it did not happen praised God accordingly. The year was 1917 and she had been praying more and more earnestly since the day in 1914 when her eldest son, my father, had gone to France with the Seaforth Highlanders. By the time I was born he had given up prayer, convinced that God could have no direct interest in Man since He allowed such obscenity as war to exist.

My grandfather's prayers were fewer than his wife's, and quiet, as were my mother's. The family said morning and night prayers each day and grace before and after meals. When time permitted, and always on Sundays, my trim-bearded grandfather 'took the Book', which means that he read a chapter of the Bible (in the Gaelic language) followed by a metrical psalm after which everyone joined in reciting the Lord's prayer. A similar ceremony took place at night. In this way the Bible was read through from cover to cover again and again. Nothing was omitted, except the fierce verses of *Psalm 109*, which includes the lines:

Set thou a wicked man over him: and let Satan stand at his
    right hand.
When he shall be judged let him be condemned: and let his
    prayer become sin.
Let his days be few and let another take his office.
Let his children be fatherless and his wife a widow.
Let his children be continually vagabonds, and beg: let
    them seek their bread also out of their desolate places.
Let the extortioners catch all that he hath: and let the
    strangers spoil his labour.

> Let there be none to extend mercy unto him: neither let
> there be any to favour his fatherless children.

As a Christian my grandmother could not bring herself to say
these verses, so bitter and full of hatred. She had figurative
interpretations of most of the other violent passages in the Bible.
The 'little ones of Babylon' who were to be 'dashed against the
stones' she understood to mean the vices which spring from
pride; but Psalm 109 stretched accommodation too far and she
preferred to pass it over as a mystery beyond her contemplation,
while still maintaining, as a staunch Free Presbyterian, that
every word in the Bible had been dictated by God to its human
author.

My grandfather was not so sure, having a more critical mind
than his wife. But for both the Bible, in Gaelic, bound in thick
black leather, was the most important book in the world, almost
the only one they possessed apart from some small collections of
Gaelic songs, the religious verse of two Gaelic writers, Patrick
Grant and Dugald Buchanan, and a fat illustrated volume of
natural history, in English. My grandfather was Christian and
enjoyed the Bible well enough but, like his two close Roman
Catholic friends, he laughed at certain religious practices in a
good-natured way and without upsetting the women folk to whom
they seemed to matter a little too much. He was aware of
inconsistencies in biblical texts; but these did not disturb his
faith in God as creator of the universe and all it contains, nor
his recognition of Jesus Christ as a loving Saviour and generally
his guide in life. He enjoyed his work as a gamekeeper, the
company of friends, whisky and good food. His eyes looked out
above his beard with kindness and humour. He was not an
enthusiast about church-going, being a tolerant person who
could not applaud sermons which denounced Roman Catholics
as idolatrous slaves of the 'Great Whore of Babylon' and
members of the Church of Scotland as 'back-sliding Laodiceans,
neither hot nor cold' whom God would spew out of his mouth.
Sincerity he respected wherever he found it. Hypocrisy and
humbug he avoided meeting as far as possible. 'Judge not that
you be not judged' was one of the admonitions in the Bible to
be taken very seriously; so he preferred to avoid rather than
confront whatever he felt to be hypocrisy. It is hardly surprising
that he never quarrelled with anyone about religion. Nor is it

surprising that my mother, coming into a community of crofters and gamekeepers whose language and customs were foreign to her, as was much of their religious outlook, found in him a staunch friend and a wonderful substitute for her own father whom she had never known. She was a member of the Church of Scotland to whom Catholicism and Free Presbyterianism were equally new, but in the ecclesiastically mixed Gaelic-speaking peasant community in Inverness-shire to which marriage and war had brought her from Caithness, there was a common spirituality which she could appreciate and share.

That spirituality was marked by awareness of the presence of God in all His creation. 'The earth is the Lord's and the fullness thereof', said the psalmist. 'How great are thy works, O Lord! thou hast made all things in wisdom; the earth is filled with thy riches.' The world was full of wonder and the glory of God, but with hints of danger for a small child, since there were adders on the moor, there was thunder among the hills, and stags seen over the garden hedge in winter were terrifying when they shook their great horned heads and galloped past. Beautiful and fascinating though God's world might be, a certain care was needed in exploring its wonders even in daytime, and then especially in the apparently unending forest where there was a continual soughing in the high pine trees and where it was so easy to get lost. Night had its own terrors, to be faced also with confidence in God's protection. The faithful would say to the Lord: 'Thou art my protector and my refuge; my God in you will I trust.' There might or might not be ghosts, witches, kelpies and other uncanny things but, said my grandmother, who tended to believe in them all, 'Put your trust in God whatever happens, and go forward: then nothing on earth or in hell will get you!'

That was the environment in which my first two and a half years were passed. Memories of it were refreshed and experience extended in later years, which included seven spent in Caithness, close by the North Sea with its bewildering changes of mood; thundering hundred foot waves against the cliffs in winter tempests, or silver and tranquil under a summer sky as brown-sailed fishing boats moved out from Wick in the evening. Always there were phrases from the Bible which fitted our experience, and people who talked to God about every detail of daily life, expressing their recognition of Him even when they swore.

We knew people in Inverness-shire like old Neil, six foot four and broad in proportion, who struggled with the Bible in English because he had never learned to read Gaelic. He was not comfortable in English, which he read for the most part as a foreign language heavy with unfamiliar words over which he stumbled. He would have been surprised to know how much he had in common with Catholic islanders on Hebridean crofts, who said the rosary in Gaelic at family prayers instead of reading the Bible. Like Neil they gave their work into God's keeping. Neil would yoke his horse to plough or reaper, remove his bonnet from his head and exclaim 'Christ be with us!' followed by 'Hup!' to the horse as he flicked the reins. He did not know the hymn 'Christ be beside me, Christ be before me.' Unlike my grandfather he avoided Catholics and never knew that he and they had anything in common beyond certain standards of hospitality, which were regarded not so much as Christian in origin but as characteristic of the Gaelic race from times beyond history.

Childhood was past when I discovered the rich body of prayers and hymns recorded in traditionally Catholic areas of the Highlands and Islands by Alexander Carmichael, and published in the volumes of *Carmina Gadelica*. One reciter in Moidart said to him: 'My mother would be asking us to sing our morning song to God down in the backhouse, as Mary's lark was singing it up in the clouds, and as Christ's mavis was singing it yonder in the tree, giving glory to the God of the creatures for the repose of the night, for the light of the day, and for the joy of life. She would tell us that every creature on the earth here below and in the ocean beneath and in the air above was giving glory to the great God of the creatures and the worlds, of the virtues and the blessings, and would *we* be dumb!' The same reciter said that her mother had taught her 'that we might clothe our souls with grace while clothing our bodies with raiment.' So there was a prayer to recite while dressing. Sometimes the children would have excuses for omission when they were late in rising and dressing. Their mother seems to have held the sensible view that heart and mind matter more than manner of speech or ceremony, and that it is better to say morning prayers while struggling into one's clothes than not to say them at all. One can at least say 'glory be to the Father and to the Son and to the Holy Spirit' in thanksgiving for the gift of another day.

The morning prayers recorded by Carmichael are longer than that, by modern standards sometimes very long, but often by any standard beautiful. They come from a people for whom there was little distinction between sacred and secular because God was present everywhere and in everything, at all times. So there were prayers for the sun's rising and at the coming of the new moon, prayers for journeys, prayers for milking, for churning, ploughing, reaping, weaving, lighting or smooring the fire, prayers to be said in sickness, prayers for childbirth, prayers for dying; prayers in fact for ever human situation. The memory of these was still faintly persistent in my grandparents' house; the old word chains had long gone but things would still be blessed in the name of the Father, Son and Holy Spirit, though without making the sign of the cross as the Catholics did. And my grandmother always went out to greet the new moon.

Among Protestants and Catholics many traces of an older belief lingered, reflected especially in the precautions they took against the fairy people and against witches. Carmichael describes the 'caim', made by Catholics and Protestants when faced with danger or anything uncanny. In making the "caim" the suppliant stretches out the right hand with the forefinger extended, and turns round sunwise as if on a pivot, describing a circle with the tip of the forefinger while invoking the desired protection. The circle encloses the suppliant and encompasses him as he walks onward, safeguarded from all evil without or within.'

The 'caim' used by Catholics differed from Protestant forms by including the saints in the invocations, especially Mary, Michael, Columba and Brigit. A good example is the following:

The holy Apostles' guarding,
The gentle martyrs' guarding,
The nine angels' guarding
Be cherishing me, be aiding me.
The quiet Brigit's guarding,
The gentle Mary's guarding,
The warrior Michael's guarding
Be shielding me, be aiding me.
The God of the elements' guarding,
The loving Christ's guarding,
The Holy Spirit's guarding,

Be cherishing me, be aiding me.

There were many prayers for protection against the unseen forces of evil. The visible world and the invisible were closely involved with each other, and even young sceptics were careful not to be too dogmatic about the latter. My agnostic father and my atheist Uncle Tom had been made uncomfortable on occasion by their mother's second-sight, and were unable to explain away ghostly apparitions seen by close friends or by members of the family. My uncle would quote *Hamlet*: 'There are more things in heaven and earth, Horatio, than are dreamt of in your philosophy', and express his faith that human science would one day find a complete explanation of such experiences. My father was reticent in the matter of witches, having been startled as a youth of fourteen by encountering one Morag and two other women crouched in a hollow of the moor at five o'clock on a summer morning as he was on his way to the farm where he worked. That alone might not have stamped itself on his mind but for the evening when a close family friend stumbled into the house white and shaken. He had been walking along the road when he saw Morag approaching. Much as he disliked her it seemed only prudent, in view of her reputation, to wish her a good evening. She looked at him without replying, and a few yards later he looked back uneasily and saw that the road was bare. 'What's the old witch up to now?' he wondered uneasily. He was not far from our house when a neighbour called from his garden, 'Did you hear that Morag died this morning?'

My father and uncles were caught between two cultures. Until they went to school they spoke only Gaelic. They knew the life of the croft, of moor and forest, river and loch. The village of a few hundred people, in whose school they were taught English and the rudiments of French and Latin, Mathematics and Science, English Literature and British History, made little impact on life around. But a maternal uncle lived in the village who kept a shop and had married a middle-class woman with English ways. My grandmother was determined that her eldest son should improve himself as his uncle had done; so my father went to London as an apprentice in a drapery firm, and his brothers in due course to London and Glasgow. My grandfather, as usual, let his wife have her way. Then the Great War came and convulsed the world, and all the young people, with few exceptions, had to leave the community. A way of life was gone; the new way would be increasingly in towns and cities, with only sparrows, starlings and pigeons to remind one of the morning song.

Yet the basic facts remained clear to some at least. God is not absent even when we turn our faces from Him. He cannot be absent, even when we sin, since it is His creative power and goodness that keeps us in being. Even in the darkest areas of a city there are those who are aware of His presence in spite of all that masks the beauty of earth and sky and destroys access to the quiet on the hills, in woods, on the sea. They find it possible to greet God in the morning and evening and at intervals during the day, at mealtimes for example. It is possible to speak to Him, or simply to be aware of His presence while cleaning vegetables or cooking, or painting and decorating. During the Second World War I knew a Polish engineer who escaped from Poland to serve with the Polish forces in Britain. He seemed always to be aware of God and to draw nearer to Him through his work of designing bridges. For him, after all he had lived through, work and prayer, prayer and living were one, as for the Highland people of my early childhood.

The old people whom I knew used many ways to direct their attention more closely to God. In Catholic households there were always crucifixes to remind them of God's love. In Protestant households there was often a copy of Holman Hunt's picture *The Light of the World* or some colourfully decorated text to catch the eye. Verses of Scripture were used as ejaculatory prayers to be thrown out according to the occasion and its need. 'God have mercy on me, a sinner!' It is good to have small prayers which can be used when going about the ordinary affairs of the day, and everyone had their own favourites, drawn from the Scriptures or the worship of the Catholic Church, sometimes composed by themselves without conscious art as they became more at home with God. I do not remember much talk about prayer when I was a small child; no more than there was about porridge and milk. Old ways had gone, new ones had come, but the fundamental practice of prayer was still the same, not least to my mother, her blue steady eyes looking calmly at the world from a quiet face.

2

We lived beside the sea, outside Wick with its 7,500 inhabitants, for less than two years, until I was approaching school age, when my father found a house two or three hundred yards from a primary school in the town. It must have been about then that my mother taught my brother David and I to kneel each night, eyes closed, hands together, and say:

> This night I lay me down to sleep,
> I give the Lord my soul to keep.
> If I should die before I wake,
> I pray the Lord my soul to take.

The Lord, we were told, was the 'Good Man' who lived above the sky. Our soul was what kept us alive here on earth, but a time would come when the Good Man would take us all to live with himself in heaven, to be happy with him forever. We did not know any bad men, not even the devil, since my mother only referred to him much later and my grandmother never spoke of him except in Gaelic. Nor did we know anyone whose soul the Lord had taken until we moved into Wick, when many things happened.

The first was Aunt Margaret's death. The telegraph boy arrived about eight o'clock one Saturday morning and my father jumped from bed crying out 'Meg's dead!' and calling for the railway timetable. There was no attempt at explanation until after he had dashed for the train, and then my mother told us that the aunt we had never seen, Dad's only sister, had gone to God. Next, Victor died. He was a boy about my own age who lived just round the corner and I had hoped to play with him. There had been no children of the same age in my life until then. Everyone was saddened by Victor's death and so my sorrow was not alone. When we walked through the churchyard sometime later, and saw the white angel statue over the grave where his body lay, they said his soul was up above, somewhere. Not knowing Victor's parents personally I could not ask them if Victor had said, each night by his bedside, 'I pray the Lord my soul to take.' It was all puzzling and disappointing.

Then David fell ill. (We were now three, and would be five—myself Ian (born 1917), David (1921), Janet (1922), Bill (1924) and Tom (1929)). David and I shared a bed, and all one night he tossed and sweated, becoming more and more excited until he was up on his knees chasing imaginary sheep out of bed and crying 'Shoo, shoo! Chase them out!' It was already day and my mother told me to dress quickly and fetch Mary Clyne, her old standby in trouble, who lived only a hundred yards away. Mary had worked on my Caithness grandfather's farm, and annually for years as a gutter at the herring fishing in Wick and Yarmouth. We loved her dearly; and her funny little cottage which had fish drying on its outside walls and inside was stacked with thousands of copies of religious magazines and tracts. They staggered against the walls, except by the fireplace, and there was scarcely room to move between them and the furniture. Mary had ginger wine with a kick to it, and ginger biscuits. The wine was hot to the throat and we imagined that Mary took it for her chest, against which she wore a rabbit skin cured by herself. Photographs of her two sons and her daughter stood on a dresser. She received letters now and again from her family, all doing well in America, but we knew that she had never been married. 'There are many like her,' said my mother, 'but Mary's a good soul and a good friend.' But she laughed and Mary laughed, and she shook her head in mild reproof, when Mary sang to us:

Little laddie, cup o' tea,
Come to bed an' cuddle me!
Put your leggie over me
An' keep my belly warrum!

At the ages of four and a half and two years we could not think what they were laughing at. 'You'll understand when you are older,' said my mother. 'That you will!' laughed Mary.

Mary was round and solid, comforting and smelt of peppermint. She cared for us as she had cared for my mother when she was a child. She stayed with us that morning while my father on his bicycle fetched the doctor. David had double pneumonia, in those days a very serious illness for anyone, but especially a small child who was already delicate. 'If it is God's will he will be taken,' said Mary, 'but pray that he'll be spared to us yet. The Lord gave and the Lord taketh away. It's in His hands.' Mary was not a member of any church and I am not sure where her many tracts came from, but she was wise and tolerant, full of broad, friendly humour and of prayer. The largest of the texts above her fireplace declared in bold letters surrounded by a flowery design 'GOD IS LOVE'. My father once remarked, 'She knows a damn sight more about it than all the clergy put together.' She and my mother took turns in nursing David night and day with skill, love and prayer. We were very quiet until the danger was past.

It may have been as a result of David's illness that a new stage in religious experience began for me. It was suggested that I might spend the summer holidays with my grandmother in Inverness-shire. The problem was how to get me there, as my father could not be spared from work for long enough and nobody would believe that I could make a journey of about 120 miles by train all by myself. I was sure I could; and at last Dad agreed that if he saw anyone on the train whom he knew, and who was willing to take charge of me, then I could go. The first walk along the platform was agony; compartment after compartment, no one. Back again, with me pulling on his hand, saying, 'I can go myself!' A friendly but unfamiliar face looked at the scene with interest and my father explained the situation, successfully. So at last the journey began, continuing without boredom until an amused guardian saw an excited small child delivered to Granny and carried off in a wagonette drawn by two black horses.

The summer was magic. The sun streamed through yellow blinds every morning while outside the hens sang their morning chorus asking for freedom and food. The pump under the apple trees was fun and I learned its mystery and was allowed to lie on my stomach and gaze down between the planks to the cool green shining depths. Lying in long grass under the trees, and keeping very still, one saw a strange green world where beetles and spiders went about their affairs unaware of the watcher, whose subsequent questions taxed a granny's knowledge of insects. Later in the day wax crayons melted to uselessness in one's hand; not that it mattered much if they did as I no longer had to play alone. On the first morning I saw, sitting on a bank in a neighbour's field, and gazing in my direction, three little girls, one of whom seemed about my age. David had been too delicate to play with and my baby sister Janet was too small, but these three were exactly right. On the occasions when it rained we all played in their house and ate their mother's scones and pancakes. Their house was very like ours, fragrant with smells of baking, of wood fires, frying bacon, honey, and well-water in white enamelled pails.

It appeared that they went to church sometimes, which I had never done. My grandmother went every Sunday, in a long black coat and a black bonnet, walking three miles there and three miles back if the farmer who normally gave her a lift in his pony trap was ill or away. She took me with her one Sunday. Everyone was very slow and solemn. When the minister began to preach, the woman in the next seat leaned over and gave me a peppermint. Everyone seemed to have sweets at that point, and when I had sucked mine I fell asleep. There was a funny smell in church like the one from our blanket chest. There were interesting lines in the varnished wood of seats and pews which could be made into faces. There was a man who stood up now and again and sang something; then all the people sang back to him. First it was all in English, and after a while everything began again in Gaelic. There was more preaching, with more sweets and I fell asleep again. Two hours was a lot for a four year old to sit still and although everyone said afterwards how good I had been it was a relief to be told that next Sunday the girls and I would stay at home together, with some older members of their family to look after us.

Next morning, lying in bed at my grandmother's back, listening to the hens and watching the sun on the blinds, I said 'I think I would like to be a minister.' 'Oh!' replied my grandmother, 'then you will have to be good!' There was silence for some moments before my next question. 'How does one be good?' She answered, 'You have to be kind to people, and say your prayers.' There was silence after that while the words were turned over in my mind. I thought 'I will be good,' but it seemed better to keep the decision to myself and God, who knew anyway everything I thought or did. In any case I did not want to be told again that I should not tease Ettie so much, or pull her pigtails, especially as Ettie was a year younger than I.

The idyllic summer came to an end in the cold air of Caithness, when I arrived back a week after the school term had begun. On my first day home I remarked casually at lunch, 'This stew is not as nice as Granny's.' My mother burst into tears;

father aimed a smack in my direction; one of the little ones—
Bill—howled. The storm raised by an innocent remark was
terrifying and inexplicable. Fortunately my mother calmed it
fairly quickly. What had happened was another of those things
one would understand when one was older. It was as well to
have some such reassurance, since it was all beyond
understanding at the time.

School was worse. It had not begun well the previous term.
The teacher did not want a new child imposed upon her by the
headmaster in the last term of the year. 'Sit there!' she snapped,
pointing to a front seat without a protecting desk in front of it.
It was exposed and lonely. The big rocking-horse caught my
eye and I liked the afternoon period when the class sang:

> I had a little pony, his name was Dapple-grey;
> I lent him to a lady to ride a mile away.
> She whipped him and she thrashed him,
> And drove him through the mire!
> I will not lend my pony more for all that lady's hire!

As the others sang, some children rode on the rocking-horse. I
longed to be one of those children, but never was. After the
summer holidays there was no hope of riding, ever, for I was in
disgrace. The teacher, whose name has remained in my mind,
gave me a public scolding for daring to return late for term. For
the rest of the year any revelation of ignorance was followed by
a reminder that boys who extended their holidays were
inevitably backward. The safest policy for most of the day was
to avoid drawing attention to oneself as far as possible. The
periods which could be enjoyed were those in the afternoons in
which we made things out of coloured paper or played singing
games out on the floor. We sang:

> Three times round went the gallant, gallant ship,
> And three times round went she!
> Three times round went the gallant, gallant ship,
> Till she sank to the bottom of the sea! of the sea,
> Till she sank to the bottom of the sea!

We also sang:

> Water, water wildflower, growing up so high,
> They are all ladies, and they must all die!

Except so-and-so, she's the fairest of us all;
She shall dance and she shall sing,
And we will make a merry ring!

while the chosen girl stood shy or smiling in the middle. A greater favourite with most children, was 'The farmer has a dog'—which concluded with everyone rushing into the centre and beating the dog!

There was singing in the morning but I do not remember much of that in the first infant class. We began the morning by reciting 'Our Father, which art in heaven,' but in the higher infant class they sang psalms every morning which could be heard clearly through the partition between our two rooms. Some were psalms already familiar, such as 'The Lord's my shepherd' and 'All people that on earth do dwell,' but there was a new and intriguing one with strange, wonderfully sounding words which I got by heart through listening to the other class:

How excellent in all the earth,
Lord, our Lord, is thy name!
Who hath thy glory far advanced
Above the starry frame.

From infants' and from sucklings' mouth
Thou didest strength ordain,
For thy foes' cause that so thou might'st
Th'avenging foe restrain.

The first verse conveyed ideas that were fairly familiar by my fifth year of life but the other verse held and teased my mind. 'Sucklings' was a new beautiful word. *We* were infants, whatever 'sucklings' might be. By questioning my parents I discovered that God apparently had a use for infants and even for babies still at the breast, that He had some use for me. It must have been about then that I began to listen carefully to stories about the child Jesus.

That fifth year was rich in new experience. One Sunday in summer my mother agreed at last to take me to her church. We sat in a gallery, right at the front where I could see the people sitting below, and straight across from us the minister stood in the pulpit, his forehead polished brightly. 'Why does his head shine?' I whispered. 'Perhaps he is hot,' replied my mother, but I could see no beads of sweat on his pink skin. But there were other things to do instead of wasting time wondering about his forehead. There were cushions on the seats and thick hassocks on the floor for people to rest their feet on. During the sermon I sat down on a hassock, hidden from view with my sweets and quietly playing a game of my own invention until everyone stood up to sing. The singing was different from my grandparents' church. There was a choir, and an enormous organ with more pipes than I could count, and instead of the psalms the people sang hymns with catchy tunes, like:

Shall we gather at the river,
The beautiful, the beautiful river?
Gather with the saints at the river
That flows from the throne of God?

and,

There is a city bright,
Closed are its gates to sin;
Naught that defileth, naught that defileth,
Shall ever enter in.

There was another hymn which I recognised at once as Happy Harry's song: 'Onward, Christian soldiers, marching as to war.' Every Sunday morning David and I rushed to the garden gate when we heard the Salvation Army band marching along the road, big banner flying above Happy Harry's smiling face, the big drum and the bugles curling our toes with delight. Harry was a tailor in ordinary life and he made my first 'real' coat out of an old one of my father's. 'How are you to-day, Harry?' people would ask. 'Happy, so happy!' Harry would answer with a broad smile. I liked Harry, and Dad said: 'The Salvation Army do a great deal of good work. Harry's honest. He's genuine. There's no hypocrisy there!' I did not know what that word meant but both parents agreed about Harry and the Salvation Army, although they themselves went to different churches and my father did not hold family prayers as his mother did. My atheist uncle said: 'When your Dad goes to church it is only to keep your Granny happy.'

Life was becoming complicated indeed. There was so much which apparently one would only understand later on; as, for example, why little boys and little girls passed water in different ways but should not do so in front of each other. On winter

nights we were bathed together in front of the kitchen fire and if
Mary was there she played castration games, holding out her
thumb between first and middle fingers of her hand and saying
'I've got your little mannie! There it is! But you can have it
back!' We knew that that was something girls did not have but
had never given it any thought. There was a bigger puzzle
connected with having a little sister, which was, where had the
doctor got her? He had brought her to our house one afternoon
when I was at a cousin's farm, but nobody seemed to know
where exactly he got the babies that he gave to people. Even
Mary didn't seem to know. She was upset when some fishermen
she knew were drowned and it was shattering to see Mary so
shaken. School was horrible much of the time. Home was good,
and the garden where my father allowed me to help and and
where David and I had a swing and planks and old wooden boxes
to play with. There were rooks in the trees at the foot of the
garden, noisy sparrows in the ivy on the walls of our house, and
the Caithness sky in summer was full of larks. It was good to go
walking out of the town over the flat Caithness land, on a Sunday
afternoon with one's parents, or to go to the sands at Reiss on
the handlebars of my father's bicycle. Mother sang often and
Dad sometimes. Although it was becoming more complex, life
on the whole was good.

3

Books attracted my attention from an early age. In my
grandparents' house they were regarded with a kind of reverence
as though something of the religious significance of The Book
was shared by other books. My grandmother would never burn
a book or tear it up; even worn-out school-books were left to
natural decay in a sort of terminal library, a cupboard set against
the west gable of her house. My father had a passion for books
and read everything and anything within reach. His books were
handled with care by himself and by my mother; for both, books

were a high road into wider experience of the world. So they were delighted when, on my third birthday, a parcel arrived addressed to me, which obviously contained a book. It was called *Our Animal Brothers*, and was an illustrated annual with a red cover produced by some animal lovers' society, or it may have been a bound volume of one year's issues of a magazine published by the society. I think now that perhaps it was the latter, but to me then it was a most exciting and tantalising possession. Now and again I was allowed to hold it and to turn the pages, as a treat. There were photographs of cats and dogs, horses and birds. Some photographs illustrated cruelty to be avoided or actively opposed. Horses should not have 'bearing reins', birds should not be killed to provide feathers for women's hats. One photograph was especially interesting when we moved to Wick, because it showed what looked like the trees at the bottom of our garden with the cluster of rooks' nests in their high branches. The picture was at the top of the left hand column on a left hand page; in the right hand column, at the top, were the words: '"Caw, caw, caw!" said the rooks as they flew to bed.' My mother read them repeatedly by request until I knew them by heart. 'I can read!' I boasted one day to a visiting uncle, moving a finger under the recognisable symbols.

School was seen as a way to reading. Sums were a nuisance taking away precious time from books. Multiplication tables were a nightmare because of the number of times I was strapped for making mistakes in their recitation; they were such a worry that I began to walk in my sleep muttering the 'seven times' table. Reading lessons on the other hand were excitement, and painful suspense at times; glimpses of the books used in higher classes filled me with eagerness to move on from the infant stage as soon as possible. Parents, grandparents and uncles were pleased by such thirst for learning, though for different reasons. My father deplored lack of interest in arithmetic and brushed aside his mother's repeated suggestion that he should teach me the Gaelic language. 'What use will that be to him?' he said. He kept a careful eye on our reading. D. C. Thomson's *Rover* and *Wizard*, and later stories by Enid Blyton, circulated among other children. 'Rubbish!' said my father, 'don't waste your time on such trash!' David and I, and then Janet, did smuggle the forbidden literature into the house occasionally, reading it at night under the blankets with a candle in a biscuit tin, but not for long, as other material caught our interest.

Natural history ranked high among our interests. Concern with birds and animals was traditional in the family and parents and grandparents had a sympathetic relationship with them, which did not exclude use of them as food. 'Three hundred years ago she would have been burned as a witch!' exclaimed Uncle Tom, watching his mother sitting at her door knitting, with the cat Cailleag at her feet blinking lazily at the birds who hopped around them both, picking up the crumbs the old lady had scattered. She kept bees. She and my father, and some of their friends, worked among them without any protective coverings and were very rarely stung. She never was, as far as I remember. She showed me how to insert a hand gently among the warm velvety bodies to help a swarm on its way, as it moved up an inclined wooden platform into a new hive. We would sit beside the hives in summer watching the busy flight and musing on the lives of insects, while Granny knitted. One school-book had a passage on the common house fly by T. H. Huxley, who described the insect as 'washing its hands with invisible soap and imperceptible water.' That made me look more closely at my mother's pet aversion! The words had a fine sound and were a joy to repeat, as were passages about ants from the *Book of Proverbs*:

Go to the ant, thou sluggard! Consider her ways and be wise; which although she hath no guide, nor master, nor captain, provideth her meat for herself in the summer and gathereth her food in the harvest.

The same writer described the ant as one of the 'four very little things of the earth that are wiser than the wise.' Scripture, natural history and personal experience came together at that stage to reinforce parental teaching about the importance of steady work, prudence and foresight. What was true of the ant and the bee was true also of our crofter friends and relations. In another way it was illustrated from my mother's experience as a hospital nurse. There was a use for everything and a place for everything. The bee and the ant worked in an orderly fashion, as father did in the garden and mother in the house. It made sense.

Verse became one of our keen interests about the same time, an interest wakened first by the metrical psalms. Although songs were also in the air they did not register as powerfully as the

psalms, as word patterns. At some point between the ages of six
and eight David and I made the great discovery that metre and
rhyme were something we might be able to handle. It was a wet
and windy day and our noses were pressed to the window pane
when a seagull swooped past blasting a large white dropping
against the glass. 'Scorrie's scoot on the window pane' one of us
cried. A few seconds later, 'He's done it once and he'll do it
again!' continued the other, and we chanted our couplet again
and again triumphantly. Dad and Uncle Tom encouraged this
new interest and there were occasions when we listened as they
read their own verses to each other, or quoted Burns and
Shakespeare or some other poet. Uncle Tom could recite the
whole of *Tam o' Shanter* by heart, his broad red face and rolling
eyes reinforcing the words. It did not matter that the meaning
of the scores of words in the poem escaped us. We were carried
along by the sound and by the feeling which inspired the
performance; the gist of the story was enough.

Soon we were exploring the Bible not only for the stories, which
had a flavour missing in the Thomson publications, but for the
sound and the colour of its words. Some parts, like the history of
David, King of Israel, had all we could desire. In bed on Sunday
mornings we read aloud the adventures of the boy David, how he
slew the giant Goliath with a stone from his sling and escaped from
the anger of King Saul with the help of his friend Jonathan, the
king's son. We mourned with him for Saul and Jonathan, and for
his rebel son Absalom, caught by the hair in a branch as he fled from
battle, and stabbed by his father's merciless general, Joab. Later, in
school, we learnt by heart the great lament for Saul and Jonathan:

The beauty of Israel is slain upon thy high places; how are
the mighty fallen!

Tell it not in Gath, publish it not in the streets of Askelon:
lest the daughters of the Philistines rejoice, lest the
daughters of the uncircumcised triumph.

Ye mountains of Gilboa, neither let there be rain upon you,
nor fields of offerings; for there the shield of the mighty
is vilely cast away, the shield of Saul as though he had
not been anointed with oil.

From the blood of the slain, from the fat of the mighty, the
bow of Jonathan turned not back, and the sword of Saul
returned not empty.

Saul and Jonathan were lovely and pleasant in their lives,
    even in death they were not divided; they were swifter
    than eagles, they were stronger than lions.
Ye daughters of Israel, weep over Saul, who clothed you in
    scarlet with other delights, who put ornaments of gold
    upon your apparel.
How are the mighty fallen in the midst of the battle! O
    Jonathan, thou wast slain in thine high places.
I am distressed for thee my brother Jonathan; very pleasant
    hast thou been to me; thy love to me was wonderful,
    passing the love of women.
As the love of a mother for her son so was my love for
    thee.
How are the mighty fallen and the weapons of war
    perished.

The Old Testament introduced us, more deeply than we could
appreciate at the time, to the complexity of man. Our hero David
was at times a thoroughly nasty type, notably when he engineered
the death of Uriah the Hittite so that his adultery with Uriah's
wife Bathsheba might not be found out. The patriarch Jacob was
a sneak who diddled his brother Esau. Our sympathy was with
Esau and not with the 'mummy's pet' who supplanted him. It
was explained to us that although Jacob was something of a
twister he had a better sense of what really mattered in life than
his elder brother, who was willing to give up his inheritance and
the responsibility that went with it for a plate of porridge! Esau
might have been tough physically but he must have been a bit of
a baby under all the muscle and hair if he could not wait a little
until a meal was ready to eat. Perhaps he hadn't meant what he
said to Jacob in the first place, which would mean that he was a
twister too! Father Abraham had not been all that admirable,
letting other men take his wife and pretending she was his
unmarried sister. We wondered what Isaac must have felt when
he realised that Abraham was about to slay him as a sacrifice to
God. Why had God allowed the good young king Josiah to be
killed by the Egyptians when He must have known that his son
and heir would do nothing but evil? And what exactly was the
dirt that came out from the belly of Eglon, King of Moab, when
the left-handed assassin thrust his knife into that fat monarch?
There was much to think about in the Bible.

While we were absorbed, by our first choice, in tales of heroism and horror in the Old Testament, our attention was steadily directed at home and at the Church of Scotland Sunday School to the New Testament, and above all to the Gospels. I do not remember when my mother first began to tell us about Jesus, usually before tea on Sunday afternoons, but I remember an illustrated book in which there was a brightly coloured picture of the healing of Jairus's daughter, and another showing the return of the prodigal son. The life of Jesus became familiar, and many of the parables which He told. Having a good memory for a story I won a prize at Sunday School for displaying a more detailed knowledge of parables and miracles than any of my eight-year-old companions. Neither at school nor at Sunday School was there any real discussion of these subjects; not that it worried me at the time since questions could always be asked at home, and in any case they were not very pressing. Years later I would hear T. S. Eliot advise an audience to *listen* first to his poems, without searching for 'meaning' in the lines. The important thing was to admit the impact of sound and imagery, to allow the poetry to communicate in its own way before attempting to analyse it and identify ideas in it. That was how we received the Bible. As a child one did not try to 'find the meaning' in its stories, still less in the overwhelming vision of Ezekiel's first chapter, or the apocalyptic vision of St John, or even in the first eight verses of the closing chapter of *Ecclesiastes*:

> Remember now thy Creator in the days of thy youth, while the evil days come not, nor the years draw nigh, when thou shalt say, I have no pleasure in them;
> While the sun, or the light, or the moon, or the stars, be not darkened, nor the clouds return after the rain;
> In the day when the keepers of the house shall tremble, and the strong men shall bow themselves, and the grinders cease because they are few, and those that look out of the windows be darkened.
> And the doors shall be shut in the streets, when the sound of the grinding is low, and he shall rise up at the voice of the bird, and all the daughters of musick shall be brought low:
> Also when they shall be afraid of that which is high, and fears shall be in the way, and the almond tree shall

flourish, and the grasshopper shall be a burden, and
desire shall fail: because man goeth to his long home and
the mourners go about the streets:
Or ever the silver cord be loosed, or the golden bowl be
broken, or the pitcher be broken at the fountain, or the
wheel broken at the cistern.
Then shall the dust return to the earth as it was: and the
spirit shall return unto God who gave it.

My parents did not interfere in any way with this reading of the
Bible, but left it to speak for itself. When we asked questions
they listened to us seriously and gave what answers they could,
without pretending that knowledge and understanding of the
Bible, or anything else for that matter, was easily won.

As soon as it was clear that we knew how to treat books with
respect, neither smudging pages nor straining bindings in any
way, we were allowed free access to any book in the house. 'If
you start a book go on to the end; finish it, however hard you
find it,' said my father. 'Look up the meaning of new words in
the dictionary.' As soon as one of us had mastered the use of a
dictionary there was a further opening of horizons. Through the
dictionary we settled the meaning of 'circumcision', which had
baffled a teacher at school. To *circumcise*, we read, meant to cut
off the foreskin, as among the Jews; *foreskin*, said the dictionary,
was the prepuce, the skin covering the glans penis. *Glans* was
the rounded end of the penis; also an acorn! *Penis* was the male
organ of coition. *Coition*, said the dictionary, means a coming
together; sexual intercourse. One of Dad's medical books
provided excellent illustrations which clinched the matter
absolutely. It was wonderful what could be discovered from the
Bible and a dictionary if one followed Dad's advice steadily. In
answer to a question he said: 'The war convinced me that
circumcision is a healthy thing and I decided that any sons of
mine would be circumcised in the interests of cleanliness.' But
that, I knew, was not why Abraham had been circumcised and
all the males of his household. Circumcision was the sign in their
flesh of the covenant between God and them. It was a strange
thought that we carried in our flesh the sign of the covenant
made with Abraham. We too, it appeared, belonged in a way to
his family and came under the covenant and the blessing.

We knew already that all mankind belonged to one great

family, descendants of Adam and of Noah. The Church of
Scotland's illustrated magazine *Lands and Peoples* introduced us
to other Christians of every race and colour. My father's set of
the Harmsworth *History of the World* not only met curiosity
about the peoples of the Old Testament, but also opened my
eyes to places and peoples beyond the pages of the Bible; Benin,
Zimbabwe, China and Japan, Incas and Aztecs and Maoris.
'There are people with religions and civilizations as good as or
better than ours.' remarked my father. Here was another
problem. If there were all these civilizations and religions over
thousands of years, how did we fit in? What happened to all the
peoples who had never heard of Christ? Where and when they
were born was no fault of theirs and it was unbelievable that
God could create people simply to send them to hell, no matter
what anyone said. Burns's satire, *Holy Willie's Prayer*, was
familiar to me from Uncle Tom's recitation at an early age:

> O Thou wha in the heaven does dwell,
> Wha, as it pleases best thysel,
> Sends ane to heaven an' ten to hell
> A' for thy glory,
> An no' for any guid or ill
> They've done afore thee.

Holy Willie's idea of God was not our idea, not even my
grandmother's, although she would not say so directly and
evaded discussion of the subject.

4

In every direction the universe was expanding and life was
growing more complicated and interesting. My mother agreed
with Coleridge's conclusion to *The Rime of the Ancient Mariner*:

> He prayeth best, who loveth best
> All things both great and small;

For the dear God who loveth us,
He made and loveth all.

To learn to love plants or animals or people it was necessary to
look and to listen carefully, to move quietly when a robin or a
blackbird was nesting or when baby rabbits were playing at the
entrance to a burrow. If you stand very still they will come to
your feet and you may even pick one up and stroke it as it lies in
your arm, ears back and nervous at first. In other countries there
were people who could make friends even with snakes and lions.
People made animals bad by ill-treating them, teasing dogs for
example, or calves. Cruelty was a very great sin against God and
most of all cruelty to children or old people, because they were
so helpless against those bigger or stronger than themselves.

My mother introduced us also at an early age to the principle
that one should love one's enemies and return good for evil, and
that we should do to others nothing that we would dislike having
done to ourselves. She believed, as did my grandmother and
most of the crofting people whom we knew, of whatever church,
that Christ comes in the stranger, in the widow, the orphan, the
sick, the homeless and the prisoner. There were no prisoners in
our world, nor did we know of any orphans in Wick; these would
come later in Inverness-shire where there were scores of
boarded-out Glasgow children. 'Inasmuch as ye did it to the least
of these little ones ye did it unto me' were Christ's words; but
where did the doing stop? He seemed to set no limits to it and
to expect one to give the very shirt off one's back.

The crofting people were generous with what they had.
Surplus milk was never sold but given freely to the old, to
travellers, to anyone who needed it, and often when it might
understandably have been kept to make more butter or crowdie
or to feed the pigs. If there was an old person nearby he or she
had a share of any baking done in the house, or any fish caught,
of eggs and vegetables. Some could, and did, make heavy
demands on the patience and generosity of their neighbours, and
then there would be a hard struggle to find Christ behind a
girning voice of an ever-grasping and ungrateful hand. Sharp
impatient words would be followed by remorse and 'God forgive
me for speaking as I did to the poor silly old creature!'
Nevertheless, caring for the old was generally seen as only right
and fitting since they in their time had cared for others and still

often did so, as far as they were able. It was impressed upon us as children that it was a privilege to be of use to an old person, and there must be no question of reward. 'If an old person tries to put money in your hand say "No, thank you!" and run away,' was what our parents said. Most of the old people in fact were interesting to talk to, and some of them were full of fun, and there were quaint things often in their rooms.

The homeless poor were another matter. They moved around the country with the seasons; homing with the approach of winter to the poorhouse at Latheronwheel in Caithness, and taking to the road again in spring. Some people saw them as rascals, sinners whose wickedness had brought them to such a pass. There were some folk in our neighbourhood who saw material prosperity as a reward for godliness and poverty as evidence of a fall from divine grace. Even those who took a kinder view were frequently hard pressed when a tramp appeared at an awkward moment, when they were under pressure already perhaps from their own family or from poor health. We children would sometimes be detailed to act as hosts, to see that the tramp's cup was refilled with tea and that he had enough sugar, or to fetch him old newspapers, which were particularly in demand, if the weather turned cold, as warm lining for clothes or as cover at night. We did not take *The Times* unfortunately; it was only many years later that I discovered that it made the best substitute for blankets of any British newspaper.

Our Presbyterian household was put to the test by one tramp in particular who had been many years on the road. Dressed in cast-off trousers, dirty shirt and torn jacket under an army greatcoat, and shod in old army boots, he trudged along the less busy roads, bundle on his back topped by a fiddle. A reddish-brown riot of whiskers fell down and forward from the tangle of hair under his soft hat. His eyes were everywhere at once and his hands as restless as his eyes. Paddy was obsequious in the presence of my father and drooled over us children. A four-year-old brother disliked him intensely after the day when Paddy offered him a penny and as the boy drew hesitantly nearer put an arm round him, drew him close, and kissed him. Paddy would talk at great length about what it had been like on the road in the old days, 'when there was plenty of boxing men and wrestling men.' He drew the character of every policeman and clergyman in the north of Scotland and would tell you to a penny what he might expect to collect in each village. Beauly he rated at a shilling and sixpence. We never heard him play his fiddle but now and again he would dance an Irish jig, whistling his own accompaniment. 'Notice how he never gives away any facts about himself,' my father once commented, 'he's a careful old rascal.' 'I don't like the smelly, slobbery old beast!' exclaimed my youngest brother. 'What God has made in His own image you must not call a beast!' snapped our grandmother. 'Keep away from him,' added my father. 'God knows what brought him to this state or what mother has broken her heart over him,' was my grandmother's final comment; 'We can at least give him a bite to eat and a cup of tea—and his old papers.' So Paddy continued to call three or four times a year. He came originally, he said, from County Tipperary. My grandmother guessed that he came from a Catholic family. I doubt if she realised, although my father did, that Paddy might have been driven to the road as the only way he could find of living with his homosexuality. He grabbed me one day when Dad and Granny were both out and tried to kiss me. 'I'll do anything for you! You know what I mean? I love you!' I froze and pushed quietly with both hands, saying, 'You'll frighten the little ones.' After that I was careful to avoid him, and said nothing about it until twenty years later when my father and I were talking about tramps we had known. 'Poor devil!' he said, 'I wonder where he died.'

Then there were the tinkers. My first meeting with them was in Caithness. In summer they were often down on the shore near our first house. In winter one family used to move into a dilapidated little house in Wick from which loud sounds of battle came on Saturday evenings to thrill passing children. When in town the tinker bairns came to school, where they were ostracised, or mocked or otherwise tormented by children crying rhymes such as 'Geordie Macafie, pees in his tea!' Two sat next to me in class, smelling strongly of stale urine. As my mother combed lice from my head I expressed fiercely the disgust in which I held the tinker boys, and the hope that soon they would go back to their caves by the shore. 'What do you think you would be like,' asked my mother, 'if you had nowhere to live but a tumbledown house, or a black tent or a cave? They have no water in that old ruin, let alone a bath. *You* would be lousy all the time, if you were as poor as they are.' She told me how a member of one tinker family, after demobilisation from the army at the end of the 1914–1918 war, had worked hard and courageously to become eventually a civil servant whose tinker origins were now invisible. My father told me a little about broken clans, dispossessed Highlanders who became the tinker people. None the less I worked hard at sums in order to move up in class and away from my tinker neighbours.

Later, in Inverness-shire, we came to know a number of tinkers who were moving up in the world, hawking fish around the countryside or trading china for rags. Our blue and yellow porridge bowls came in exchange for bundles of old clothes, and on Sunday evenings the shrewd, pleasant old woman who ran the business could be seen in church as well-dressed as anyone there. Report said that she always put half-a-crown into the collection plate at the door, which placed her in the higher reaches of village society, at least financially. She showed no social ambition as far as fashionable entertainment went. 'A nice sensible woman,' said my mother, 'and a pleasure to talk to. No spiteful gossip in her conversation. We can all learn a lot from her.'

Gossip had no place in my mother's conversation either. To pass judgment on other people in her presence was even more rash than doing it in my grandmother's hearing; to label people good or bad smacked to her of blasphemy. She was firm and clear that certain actions were wrong and to be avoided at all costs, but definitive judgment of those who did them was to be left strictly to God. There had been enough skeletons in her own family cupboard to make her aware how deceptive human appearances can be.

My grandmother agreed in principle about the fallibility of man's assessment of his fellow human beings, but her objection to attacks on character was not based entirely on Scripture, as I was to discover one day after we had moved back to Inverness-shire. Having come home from school one afternoon, I vented contempt for a boy who had stood with tears rolling down his chubby face because he was unable to translate a simple Latin sentence. Annoyance was plain on my grandmother's face. 'You might remember that he is your cousin!' Aghast I replied, 'Surely we're not related to *him*!' and was rewarded by a genealogical torrent which left no doubt that we were fourth cousins. Before bedtime that day I had to face up to the fact that as a result of my father's family having lived in the same corner of Inverness-shire for at least three hundred years it was more than likely that we were related demonstrably to everyone around, except Catholics, the aristocracy, and those newcomers who had arrived in the district during the previous hundred years. The imagination reeled as cousin after cousin was identified and social assumptions were shattered.

My parents had had to learn to accept and tolerate each other's families, no easy achievement since each family had deplored their marriage and considered itself superior to the other. One grandfather was a large farmer by Highland standards, the other a gamekeeper with a croft. One family owned considerable town property, and my great grandparents on that side had once provided lunch for the future King Edward VII at their hotel, when he came to open a bridge over the River Wick. That piece of history made little impression on my father's people who disapproved of Edward anyway and regarded my mother's folk, for all their property, as inferior to themselves in most respects that mattered. Apart from any other consideration, all Caithness people were aliens to them, a collection of foreigners ignorant of Gaelic and with low standards of sexual morality illustrated by my maternal grandfather and the dairymaid and by his brother, who had left a wife and two small children and run away to South America. It made matters worse that my mother's family belonged to the Church of Scotland and that its men were usually Freemasons. On my father's side everyone was an adherent of the Free Church or the Free Presbyterian Church, except for my breakaway uncles, who had no use for masonry, which they regarded as childish, or for the Church of Scotland which they regarded as an example of intellectual and moral compromise, past and present, above all at the time of the Clearances. Memory of the Clearances coloured deeply my father's political thinking and his social outlook. One day on the hills we stood and looked across a glen to a wide green patch on the other side, among heather. 'There was a township there once,' he said grimly. We were proud of the Ross women who had resisted the authorities in Glen Calvie.

In my mother's family there was no such memory, although their women had been valiant in another way, coping with a succession of weak, spoiled men. Her women folk pitied the girl who had 'gone to the heather', where water ran outside but rarely

inside houses. They were horrified at the thought that she was
going to live on the top of a hill, two miles from the nearest
village, in a house without running water, hot or cold, among
people who spoke Gaelic to each other all day. Fortunately my
parents loved each other deeply and my mother became the
dearest of daughters to an originally hostile mother-in-law.
Except in our house members of the two families never met, but
we learned to be at home with either.

Christ came to us in them also, though it was often difficult
to remember that, especially when Grandaunt Jean on her
annual holiday tried to impose Victorian patterns of behaviour
on us, with such maxims as 'children should be seen and not
heard' or 'children should speak when they are spoken to, and
not before!' Where was Christ in her? And where was Christ in
our neighbour old Barbara, as she stood at the bottom of her
garden and shouted to another neighbour: 'I wish I was God,
and I'd send you to Hell!' 'Poor soul!' said my mother, 'she has
had much to put up with in life. I doubt if she means all that
she says.'

One way and another we were taught to regard everyone with
respect, to look for the good in people, not to speak disparagingly of
them behind their backs, and to be helpful when the occasion arose,
without expecting any reward. My awkward attempts to be helpful
in the house and garden were undoubtedly a trial to parents but
were not rejected. Instead my father showed me what I could do
usefully, and when I was eight gave me a patch of ground for myself
and two shillings with which Mary Clyne and David and I went to a
nursery to buy seeds and plants. A year or so later my mother
taught me to bake, after a disastrous experiment on my own which
produced some dirty grey rubbery discs instead of golden brown
pancakes. Effort was not discouraged, except when I tried to sing
and imitated my grandmother's Gaelic crooning so successfully
that any further effort in that direction was frowned upon for a
time; it sounded too much like mocking her, as it provoked laughter
among the listeners. It was wrong to hold anyone up to ridicule,
whether friends, relations, school-fellows, tramps or tinkers or
total strangers, especially if they suffered social, physical, or mental
handicap. The less responsible people were for their handicaps, the
more were we answerable to God for our treatment of them.

It was not easy to put these principles into practice. Even a
child could see the struggle in father and grandmother when

entertaining certain relations by marriage or meeting certain
neighbours, and how silent and non-committal mother became
when Grandaunt Jean was voicing her social prejudices. It was
difficult to be patient with some people and it was not until the
latter years of his life that my father was able to suffer fools
gladly. Grandaunt Jean however was not present all the time to
strain patience and understanding. In any case there was a
feeling that one's parents were behind one in any encounter with
the outside world, whether it was school, tramps or family
visitors. The acute problems were within our own home, where
people we usually relied upon could become a severe trial,
showing at times a hurtful lack of understanding. At times
indeed they appeared plainly unjust and very dim.

My earliest memory of that kind of adult weakness goes back
to when I was two years old and my mother and I were living
with my grandparents in Inverness-shire. There had been heavy
rain during the night and early morning; a large clear pool lay
on the garden path in front of the living-room window. The
strong sun had come out, raindrops sparkled on the bells of a
fuchsia bush by the window, gravel at the bottom of the pool
was bright with colour. I felt good. Then I found an old
scrubbing brush somewhere and the feeling of goodness became
active benevolence. In a few minutes the milking stool was
dragged from the cowshed and I was busily scrubbing it in the
pool of rainwater, only to have it snatched away by an
unexpectedly disapproving grandmother who did not appreciate
that the stool was being cleaned.

The next example of adult misunderstanding was more
serious, involving as it did my baby brother and a suggestion
that I wished to murder him. Admittedly the arrival of a brother
had been disconcerting after more than two years as the
unchallenged centre of a small secure world. His arrival was
disappointing as he could not play and was so delicate that he
had to be approached with even more care than Grandaunt
Jean's antique china teapot. About the time he was born we
moved to the house by the sea, away from the familiar house
and garden high above the Beauly Firth between moor and
forest. The new garden was not very interesting and one summer
afternoon boredom descended heavily. David's pram was
standing in the sun, a high old-fashioned perambulator whose
wide handle suddenly looked perfect for swinging on; and so I

swung on it. Over went the pram and baby and all. His yells
were hideous. Mother rushed out alarmed and then angry; as
she snatched up the little victim of acrobatic experiment I fled
from her wrath, out of the garden and across a neighbouring
field. It seemed then, and it does even now, that hours passed
before I was able to negotiate, with tears and from a canny
distance, the terms of a safe return to the house and tea.

Certainly siblings were hard to love at times, and a little sister
could be as troublesome as a little brother. One afternoon in
Wick David and I, now playing happily together, wished to go
down to a field by the riverside which had gloriously long grass
in which to hide. Jan, aged four, was determined to come with
us. 'You boys are being unkind to your little sister' was the adult
comment when we firmly refused to accept a nuisance who
would want us to make daisy or dandelion chains all afternoon.
'Take her with you,' said mother in a tone to end argument,
'but keep well away from the water's edge.' Fifteen minutes later
Jan was sitting in a shallow pool, her new tussore silk frock
floating round the miniature Ophelia and, it seemed to us, a
smug self-satisfied expression on her pretty little face. We had
made the mistake of telling her ourselves to keep away from the
water. She clambered out without needing much help from
David or me. Not for the last time I experienced the injustice
that so often burdens the eldest child in a family. We entered
the kitchen, and after one horrified glance I was seized and put
across my mother's knee, attempts to explain rapidly giving way
to tearful cries as her hand rose and fell upon my bottom. 'It's
not fair!' I protested later, again not for the last time, 'how could
I stop her? If I'd hit her that would have been wrong too!' My
two school friends, Willie Simpson and Jimmy Richards, being
also eight years of age, agreed with me that it was best for the
three of us to stick together and avoid becoming involved with
little brothers and sisters. Dad seemed to think that this was not
such a bad idea on the whole, although pointing out that the
younger ones could not be ignored at home and would have to
be considered in whatever went on there.

It was becoming clear that grown-ups were not always right.
One knew that teachers could make mistakes; everyone said so.
Adults who were not teachers also made mistakes. It was
startling to see a man munch dandelion leaves when we were
out for a walk one day. 'You'll see, they are not poisonous!' he

said to mother, whom he had overheard warning us against
them. 'It seems I was mistaken,' she remarked afterwards, 'but
it is best to be on the safe side when you are not sure of
something.' Father agreed, and there was a general discussion
about plants and berries and how to discover from specialists
what was safe and what was not. If we did not know a specialist
there were books which would be helpful. Did we know any
specialists, we asked. It seemed that we did. Mary Clyne for
example was a specialist on what could be eaten from the sea;
fish, shellfish and even certain kinds of seaweed. The doctor
was another specialist. 'You might become specialists in
something yourselves one day,' we were told. It was only long
after childhood that I discovered how easy it is to be saluted as
a specialist if the ignorance of those around is greater than one's
own. 'The wise man,' said an uncle, 'is aware of his own
ignorance. The more he knows, the more he sees there is still to
know.' It was soon to dawn on me that this was not only true of
the universe around us, but also of people and our knowledge of
them.

5

A critical point in relationships with people came at the end of
my ninth year. It had been clear for some time that something
unusual was in the air. There were long, serious, and sometimes
tearful discussions involving parents, grandmother, uncles and
various friends, but only occasionally and briefly overhead by us
children. My grandmother's voice decided the issue; that
summer we moved to Inverness-shire. My father had been
persuaded against his own better judgement to launch a business
there in partnership with his youngest brother, whose ideas were
sound but whose business methods were to prove chaotic. We
were to move in stages. Father and the three eldest were to stay
with his mother until we could move into our new house in the
village, where my mother and two younger brothers would join

us some weeks later. It was all exciting and the prospect of being closer to my lively and poetic uncle was welcome. We loved Uncle Tom, and never had enough of his company. Like my father, he was about five feet eight inches in height, but stout and bluff in manner, with a cheerful red face and a rolling gait, explained by the fact that a childhood injury had left one leg shorter than the other. He made people smile or laugh as soon as they met him. He more than anyone else encouraged efforts to write verse and to make up adventure stories, was endlessly entertaining, and a great favourite with us children.

New house, new school; the house was satisfactory enough but the school was alarming. The town primary school had been a quiet place where fights were rare and strongly discouraged by corporal punishment of these involved. The village school, with about 230 children between the ages of five and fourteen was ceaselessly in motion; the children seemed to explode with crazy energy and to be always fighting, rarely angrily but always as though their lives depended on throwing themselves totally into any contest. I felt out of place, with a Caithness accent and a timid nature, and showed this plainly at home. That was why the statement that I felt unwell one Friday morning was dismissed as an attempt to avoid school. Vomiting on Friday and on Saturday was explained away as the result of eating berries from the hedge on the road from school. No denial of berry eating had any effect on adult attitudes beyond producing a sermon on lying from my grandmother. Vomiting was accompanied by a constant pain. The week-end became a timeless nightmare. On Monday morning Uncle Tom looked in and gave me his strong support, and a lift to school in his car. 'The child is obviously ill,' he said. My father agreed that if I felt no better I should go to the doctor during the morning break.

The quarter mile walk from school to the doctor's house was slow and black with pain. Minutes later I was in a hired car on the way to hospital in Inverness, my father silent and white-faced beside me, his eyes moving unhappily from the window to me and back again. Whooping cough, chickenpox, chilblains, measles, earache and toothache had come and gone; a hand scalded by boiling porridge; this pain was different from anything and made worse by the hopelessness of trying to describe it to father and grandmother. It was an immense relief to be in the hands of doctors and nurses. As Nurse Tuach painted my stomach with iodine, or something like it, she smiled and remarked cheerfully, 'We are going to take you to the theatre to see Charlie Chaplin.' She looked taken aback by the retort: 'No, nurse. I'm going to have an operation, because if I don't I'll die.' That fact was clear in my mind, and I thought about death as preparation went on and as the trolley rolled towards the operating theatre. It seemed simple and a little exciting. Everything died. If there was no God, as Uncle Tom said, and one became only a handful of dust, there was nothing to fear. If there was a God, as mother and grandmother said, He was good and one would be happy with Him. Either way pain and tears would be over. The chloroform pad came down; there was a whirring of countless wheels in my head as I went under, to surface hours later without my appendix. When my mother arrived from Wick there was news only of a successful operation.

Post-operational treatment of appendicitis is much better now than it was then, when you might spend weeks in bed as I did, waiting for a wound to heal completely. The fortnight in the Royal Northern Infirmary in Inverness is unforgettable. I dearly loved Nurse Tuach, her smile and smell and voice, and her way of explaining things like enemas. It helped to know what was happening. She could be trusted. And in the bed on the right was Mr Rae, from Bruce Gardens, Inverness. He and Nurse Tuach let me watch when his wound was being dressed. It was much bigger than mine but he said that he was not nearly so ill as the thirteen-year-old boy on the other side of the ward, who had a tube in his side and moaned in his sleep. Mr Rae said there were always folk in worse trouble than oneself and because of them we ought to try to put up with our pain as well as we could. So when the stitches and clips were being removed from the wound, and little bits of me with them, I kept my eyes on him and gripped the head of the bed tightly with both hands as he had showed me when his stitches were coming out.

The fortnight in hospital was followed by weeks at home before going back to school. They were brightened by my two little brothers, one in his fourth year, the other a baby I had been presented with on the morning of my ninth birthday. He had been born during the night and I was aware of much movement in the house and was sure at odd moments that my mother's voice was crying out in pain. There she was in the morning lying in bed smiling, with the new baby beside her. Bits and pieces of conversation overheard began to make sense and one took sharper notice of remarks about so-and-so having had a 'hard time with her first.' Everything fell neatly into place the following spring and summer. One day when I was exploring the countryside a farmer called for a helping hand as he toiled with a ewe in labour, and while he held her head I pulled at the legs of the emerging lamb and shared his satisfaction when the small creature lay alive and well on the ground. It was with a feeling of ripe experience that I listened some weeks later to the girl I played with from a neighbouring farm. She tumbled from her bicycle one afternoon flushed and breathless. 'They've just chased me from the byre but not before I saw what was happening. There was a calf, I'm sure, coming out of the cow!' She looked at me: 'I think that's the way we are born!' 'I'm sure it is,' was my nonchalant reply; 'I was helping Munro with a ewe the other week, and that's how the lamb was born.' We talked some more then about the ways of bulls and cows, horses and mares, and went to our respective homes well content. It seemed we had always known these things, but they had become more interesting lately. Certain passages in the Bible suddenly took on a clearer meaning, for example in the first two chapters of Genesis where it speaks of Adam 'knowing' his wife. It began to seem, too, that grown-ups were talking more freely.

We were told that, as the Book of Genesis says, everything comes to us from God, including our minds and bodies, male and female. We have dominion over most of His gifts but must respect their nature and we are answerable to Him for the use we make of them. We need to learn to understand and care for ourselves and each other if we are to grow in knowledge of God. If we do not love the brother we see, St John said in a letter, how can we love God whom we do not see? In spite of their more subtle theological differences most of the older members of the family seemed to agree that a main concern in life must be to learn, to understand, in order to be able to control and use wisely as many of our own powers as possible. We watched babies dribble at both ends, were reminded of our nappy days and of toilet training, and were sorry for a little girl whose mother sat her on a pot and left her there tied to a table leg until she gave satisfaction. People learned a certain control of bladder

and bowels, control over legs and arms and the use of speech.
People had to learn to cope with their own moods and not to
make life miserable for other people with them. Esau was soft
really, because he thought he should get what he wanted without
ever having to wait for it. It was worth waiting and working for
good things. That was why one studied or practised. Nobody
will ever be really good at anything, said my parents, without
hard work. It was plain that their own work was rewarding. In
house or garden each knew exactly what to do and how to do it;
work was done in the minimum time without fuss or bother. As
a result there was always plenty of spare time for reading or
talking or for fun, or simply to sit or lie and look. Sex was one
more part of life to be studied and controlled in the interest of
one's own happiness and that of other people. It could be used
thoughtlessly and selfishly with little respect for oneself or
others. 'A difference between us and the other animals,' said
one of the grown-ups, 'is that they are driven blindly by their
feelings while we can understand what is happening and control
ours. A dog can't resist a bitch in heat; a man can, if he wants
to.' Control was not always easy by any means, but not
impossible if one had plenty of interesting things to do and to
think about, and one could turn to God for help with any
problem and talk to Him about it. Only, often, as the Psalmist
said, He did not seem to listen. If He did listen then too often
that seemed to be all He did. 'He has His own time,' said my
mother and grandmother.

As for people: the best of them could let you down, and you
would let them down, without intending to do so. It was foolish
to put one's trust in Man. The Bible said so, and by the age of
ten I knew it to be true and found also how possible it was to
fail others even when one loved them. Selfishness came so easily
to control one's actions, especially when nobody was looking and
one could leave a mess without clearing it up, or snitch biscuits
or cake from the tins in which they were kept. It was difficult
and often confusing; and it was a relief to turn to games, to
reading, and to exploring our own neighbourhood. There was a
popular game called Relieve-O! a kind of Prisoner's Base
played in an old overgrown gravel pit with steep sides, which
lay behind the school. It released the adrenalin and banished
thought of everything except survival. It was odd how you tore
through the bushes when chased by another team, without

feeling any pain even when the brambles ripped your legs until blood poured down. It was odd also how possible it was to become so deeply absorbed in a book that one saw and heard nothing of what went on around. Such abstraction sometimes led to trouble, failure to hear an order being misunderstood as intentional disobedience. Similarly there could be awkwardness as a result of thinking. If you walked along deep in thought you could fail to notice where you were going. Once, in a shop, I was startled to hear the assistant say 'You must go to the butcher if you want mince!' Looking round in surprise I saw three grinning customers and shelves of bread and cakes.

Pain, sex, thought; all important, all to be studied and mastered by me. Me? Made by God 'in his own image and likeness,' whatever that might mean. God? 'A spirit infinite, eternal, and unchangeable: in his being wisdom, power, holiness, justice, goodness and truth.' That we had learned already in school, from the *Shorter Catechism*. It sounded beautiful, but what did it mean? That question became less pressing than another—'Who am I?,' which struck me forcibly one night somewhere in my twelfth or thirteenth year.

I was on my way to the farm to fetch milk. It was a keen winter night, the sky full of stars, the hills looming dark on the horizon, wild geese noisy on the salt marshes by the river. A few yards to the right of the road were two standing stones. 'Druid stones' the people called them. I stood opposite the stones and as I gazed at them called to mind all I had ever heard about Druids and even earlier people who had lived on the moor thousands of years before I was born. Then my eyes turned to the stars. There was much about them in *The Children's Newspaper*, which came to our house every week. Stars, planets, other worlds, millions upon millions of years away. I closed my eyes and inwardly looked at the stars and the stones, at the shadowy hills. The sound of the geese alone broke the frosty silence. How strange that I should stand with the thought of centuries dead priests and scholars in my head; images there too of stones and stars, although my eyes were closed. It was possible to shut out the sound of the wintering geese and to think only of their long flight from the North and the purpose of their travel. I stood alone in the night and the question came: 'But who am I with all this, and the stretch of time in my mind?' and I said my name silently to myself several times. 'What does that mean?'

and the answer came: 'So many pounds weight, so many feet and inches in height, curly auburn hair and blue eyes.' The idea came: shut out consciousness of body, of stones, hills, geese, dead men and distant planets with possible inhabitants: think only of me, this 'I' who looks at them all, and at his own thoughts and pictures, his body and his name: then think of nothing. The withdrawal inwards progressed slowly to a terrifying moment; shuddering I whispered my name aloud and opened all my senses wide to the world around. It was very cold and I ran with a light heart to the warmth and mingled smells of cows and paraffin lamps in the byre. It was good to be alive and to be me, even though I did not know myself all that well and was misunderstood by other folk. It was hard to know what they were after, much of the time. No wonder it was so difficult to be clear about God. There was mystery everywhere, hard to put into words. One could only look and feel, sing to oneself in secret, and try to make verses. Poetry began to carry me away, and Uncle Tom without comment introduced me through records to Mozart and Bach. He and his wife never spoiled the evenings by talking about music.

6

It must have been about the same time that a primitive fear was set at rest. There were many stories of ghosts, witches and other spooky wonders told by the fireside in our community. One of the most accomplished storytellers was Kate, and her most impressive story was about the 'Black Dog of Tomich,' impressive because Tomich was close to my grandmother's house.

'At the time this happened,' Kate would begin, 'I was working at the farm, and every morning I had to carry milk up to the big house. It was one summer morning about half past five that I was going up the drive with a pail of milk in each hand and thinking what a grand day it was going to be, and through the lime trees on the right hand side I saw the dog. It was coming out of the fir trees on the far side of the lawn and at first I thought it was Bran from the farm out for his morning walk and I whistled to him. But he didn't come running. He came on dead slow and steady and I saw that he was a lot bigger than Bran and black all over. Well, he came through the lime trees till I could see his eyes, red as fire he looked at me and then crossed in front and went into the trees on the other side. It was all I could do to get to the house, I was that frightened. The housekeeper gave me a dram and a good strong cup of tea, and I felt better, and thought maybe she was right, and it was just some stray dog after all.

'It was maybe a week later that I saw it again, coming through the trees the same way and over the grass, dead slow, and stopping to stare with its burning red eyes before it crossed the drive and disappeared in the trees on the other side. Well, I dropped the pails and ran screaming to the house and fell in a faint when the housekeeper opened the door. They got the doctor and he said it was shock. I was two days in my bed, and I would have given up if it wasn't that the job was a good one and I had to keep it. But for a while I got Alec out of his bed to go with me to the farm, though he was only four at the time, but even having a bairn with me was some comfort, for I couldn't face that drive alone. Anyway I never saw the black dog again, but one of the men did that was in the bothy on your Granny's side of the wood. He left the half-door open in the summer, for the bothy used to get hot and stuffy at night. His own dog slept on the floor near the foot of the bed and it was its whimpering that wakened him one morning. It was pointing at the door and all its hackles were up and he'd never seen it so feared before. He got up himself and looked over the half-door. There was the black dog, going along by the side of the trees.

'We kept what we had seen to ourselves but we knew that when the dog came three times it meant death in the family at Tomich. Well, sure enough, that very autumn they were building stacks at the Mains and the son—they had only one and he was sixteen at the time—fell off a high stack and broke his neck and died. The family sold Tomich after that and the black dog hasn't been seen from that time to this.'

That was Kate's story and her son remembered how she had got him out of bed to give her company on the walk from the farm to the big house. By the time I was eleven or twelve I knew the story by heart; so there was scant enthusiasm on my part when my grandmother, with whom I was staying at the time, asked me to go to Kate's house one October night to cancel some arrangement about laundry. The road to Kate went along the side of Tomich wood at one stage and fear of meeting the black dog daunted me 'Don't be silly! You're a big boy now,' was my grandmother's unsympathetic rejoinder, so away I had to go on this half-mile journey.

The first part of the way presented no problem. The second part was over a sandy track sunk between the moor on the right and the wood on my left. The night was windy. There was a moon, but masses of cloud were driven wildly about the sky and covered its face except for fleeting intervals. The wind soughed through the pine trees and I walked along wishing I had a torch, and peering nervously and stupidly into the darkness of the wood, only occasionally glancing up at the edge of the moor. Suddenly I saw the dog. It stood as big as a six-month-old stirk on the moor's edge, its head pointing north, away from me, and moving slightly as though it was searching for something out on the moor. I stood, too stiff with fright to run. A shudder ran through me at the thought of its fangs on the back of my neck if I turned and ran for home. So there we stood. It showed no sign of moving on. My mind began to work again. 'Whatever happens put your trust in God and go forward; then nothing in earth or in hell can get you,' my grandmother had said after an evening of eerie stories. Slowly and carefully I raised my left foot and put it down quietly on the sandy road, then my right; left again, a few inches forward, then the right, hands tightly clenched and my eyes never leaving the figure of the dog. Slowly I moved my arms up until they formed a cross over my chest, and then we were level, he and I. The next step would put him at my back and the hair rose on the nape of my neck as I thought of the leap the dog might make upon my back. Left foot rose and went down, and inwardly I asked God for courage, and protection from this 'terror by night'. Slowly I raised my right foot; the wind rushed with a sudden roar among the pines, the clouds went from the moon's face, and the black dog burst asunder, waving in two parts against the sky. Presently I went forward and climbed the bank, to look more closely at the bush of broom which darkness and a nervous imagination had transformed into the Black Dog of Tomich.

There seemed no point in mentioning the experience to anyone at the time and inviting laughter at my expense. Panic and flight at the first glimpse of the dog would have started debate as to what I had perhaps seen, and might have added another paragraph to Kate's story. The experience showed me the importance of taking time to look for explanations of strange phenomena at a simple level, and in later years many ghost scares were lifted from other people by close examination of shadows or acoustics. Faith had given me the courage to go forward, but it was fear which had kept me standing still in the first place instead of running away. Faith had taken a grip on fear once the first shock was over, and made it possible to face the situation and so discover how simple it really was. Long afterwards I read with a smile of recognition St Thomas Aquinas's advice to look first for a natural explanation of any vision or other unusual experience, instead of jumping to assumptions of supernatural or preternatural activity.

There were experiences of fear in other contexts, of other kinds of fear, about this date. We children were like our father in having quick tempers, which usually were fairly well controlled by the time we were entering our teens. We would kick stones instead of each other when in a rage and shout abuse instead of throwing solid objects when we quarrelled. One day, however, in the school playground there was an explosion of anger which was different. It was a wet day, the playground in places deep in mud, and a bigger boy was pestering me. As a climax to his programme of annoyance he picked up a wet cloth cap which had been trodden into the mud and threw it in my face. It was my first experience of seeing red. He ran laughing, being faster than I, but at last he stopped and I caught up, and blind with fury, hurled myself at him. Surprised by the force of the attack he fell backwards with my hands on his throat. His face was desperate and turning purple before some other boys pulled me off. I wanted to kill him. Nobody pestered me again but I was alarmed by my own violence and realised that it was necessary to control my temper more effectively. Two decisions followed which were not entirely consistent. The first was never to fight again in earnest but to learn to turn the other cheek. The second, which came a little later, was to learn to wrestle as a way of self-defence which would cause no injury to others. Wrestling soon proved a very good way of working off aggressive feelings. An old edition of *Chambers Encyclopaedia* had an article on the sport, with illustrations of a dozen holds, which a good-natured bigger boy allowed me to practise on him. As skill in wrestling grew there was little occasion to turn the other cheek and only one instance remains in my memory when I did exactly that, and made a friend.

The darkest fear came with our mother's illness. She and my father were seldom even slightly ill and we took their presence at the centre of things for granted. Then one morning we were suddenly told that we could not see her. The doctor came and went several times, and another doctor with him. Granny came, and we sat with her in the living room very quiet. Mother was too ill to be moved to hospital we were told, and a surgeon was coming from Inverness to operate on her in the house. Time became a blur, but at last they were all gone except for a nurse. We crept to bed. There in the warmth and the darkness David and I cried at last, afraid that our mother was about to die. Our prayers that night were in our own words. Mine always were, after that, except for the 'Our Father'.

Mother got better but she was never to regain her full health. She should have had a long convalescence, but the operation had been costly, in those days before the National Health Service, and there was no money to pay for convalescence. She grew quieter, and would sometimes sit gazing silently at sky or hills for a long time. Granny helped for a time in caring for us all, father and five small children ranging from eleven to two years in age, but she went back to her cottage as soon as my mother felt she could cope with work herself.

Foreboding grew in my mind. During the day it was usually forgotten in the round of school and games and household jobs. It was in bed at night that fear came and I cried over our mother's death and implored God to let her live for our sakes and not to take her yet. It was difficult to know how she was, as she never complained, but you could see that she was often very tired and found us children difficult to manage. There was no secret about one source of anxiety. My father and uncle had found their business partnership unworkable and it broke up. Most of the capital in it was my uncle's; we found ourselves suddenly poor. There was no more pocket money, no holidays, no trips to the cinema in Inverness. Housekeeping money was reduced by sixty per cent. There was no more chocolate on

Sunday afternoons and we began to eat margarine instead of butter.

One morning about two years later I went down to the kitchen at half past seven and found my mother stirring porridge. Her greeting was oddly vague and her action listless. Standing beside her I noticed that there was very little oatmeal in the pan. 'Isn't the porridge too watery?' I asked. 'Is it?' she said with a puzzled look on her face. A moment later she put her hand to her head and mumbled something, then slid to the floor, with me trying to break her fall and shouting for my father. In a few moments she opened her eyes and said 'I must have fainted.' The doctor, came, thought she had most probably a touch of influenza, and prescribed a few days in bed.

At mid-day we were startled by my grandmother's arrival on the doorstep, startled because only the day before she had gone to spend a fortnight with her nieces in Glenurquhart. 'Who is ill?' she asked. 'Nobody is really ill,' replied my father; 'Jessie has a touch of flu; but how did you know?' There was a silence. She looked upset. At last she answered: 'I had a dream last night.' She would not describe the dream but later our cousins gave their account of what happened. She had come down to breakfast that morning dressed for travel, suitcase in hand. An astonished niece, hastily casting around in her mind for ways in which she might have given offence, asked what was wrong. 'I had a dream last night. I was standing by the river and two horses came along, one brown and one white. They fought. The white horse killed the brown one in the river. There is death in Beauly, and I must go home.' Nothing would alter her decision and so she arrived on our doorstep and insisted on staying overnight.

Next morning we watched from the living room window as mother was carried into an ambulance. She was in a coma, we were told. Next day she regained consciousness for a moment and asked the nurse if the bairns were all right. Days followed with no change, but one morning we were sent home from school. There was no sign of Dad, but Granny was there. 'Take the Book,' she said to me, 'and read from St. John's Gospel, the fourteenth chapter.' I began to read: 'Let not your heart be troubled. You believe in God, believe also in me. In my Father's house there are many mansions. If it were not so I would have told you, and thither I go to prepare a place for you. And if I shall go and prepare a place for you, I will come again and take you to myself; that where I am you also may be.' It was enough. We were all in tears except Jan, who sat by the white geranium in the window as she was to do for most of that day and the next, staring silently at everyone and rarely moving. Weeks later David and I lost her rubber ball and she burst into a terrifying paroxysm of sobbing which shook her body and sounded as though it would never stop. 'The ball,' she gasped at last in Granny's arms, 'Mum gave me the ball. It was Mum who gave me it.'

My father lay in darkness day and night on a sofa in the sittingroom without eating, only occasionally drinking a cup of tea. We children did not see him until the day of the funeral. It had been decided that we should not see our mother dead and that her body would not be brought home. Instead we would meet the hearse where the road to the Old Churchyard at Kilmorack leaves the A9. It was a hot day in June. David and I were with our father in a car immediately behind the hearse. We watched the coffin moving slowly in front of us. The sound of many cars moving at walking speed was hypnotic and increased a feeling of unreality. Dad looked now and then at our set faces. None of us spoke. At the graveside I wanted the minister to stop talking so that we could go away. It was my thirteenth birthday; my youngest brother was four the previous day. My father was forty-three, my grandmother seventy-five. I did not realise then how much their lives had centred on our mother and how much dislocation would follow her death.

The night she died my father had a dream. About two o'clock in the morning Granny heard him moving and got up to see what was the matter. He was looking at the clock on the landing. 'I've had a strange dream,' he said; 'my father came into the room carrying a lighted lamp and I went to take it from him. "No, son" he said, "Leave me the lamp. I have a journey to make to-night."' My grandmother was silent a moment as they stood in their night clothes, looking at the clock. 'It is over then,' she said. It was just about then that my mother passed away.

There was a family consultation after the funeral. What was to be done with the children was the heavy problem. My father could not afford a housekeeper, even if one could be found. It looked as though we were to be divided, two, two and one, between uncles and aunts. David and I might go to the Queen

Victoria School in Dunblane, a military style establishment for
the sons of soldiers. My grandmother's contribution to the
consultation was the final one. 'The children must not be
parted.' 'How the hell can I keep them?' snapped my father.
'Who would take on the job of looking after us for the small
wage that I can offer?' He was not much relieved by his mother's
reply that she would do what she could until he found a
housekeeper or married again, but on condition that all six of us
went to live with her. The village school would admit my
youngest brother although he was under age, and so five days a
week between 8.15 am and 4.30 pm we would all be out of the
way. The walk to school was over a mile each way but in bad
weather the two little ones might be driven there, at least in the
morning. So once again we moved, out into the country.

For my father the centre had fallen apart. He had lost his wife
and his business almost simultaneously, and had to find a way
of supporting himself and us. As children we did not appreciate
the courage and humility with which he launched into business
as a travelling draper. He had no capital to start again in any
other way. It was 1930 and at his age there was no prospect of
employment. He had to survive somehow as self-employed; he
did, but the strain was great on him and on us. Business, the
vegetable garden, the fishing, took all his attention and he had
little time or patience for us. It was fortunate that we had got to
know him and love him in happier days. As it was, his
impatience and unpredictable bursts of violent anger were
hurtful, and to the younger ones utterly puzzling, but they did
not destroy the deeper bonds between us.

Much of the strain on everyone was caused by the change in
living conditions. My grandmother's cottage consisted of four
small rooms. She and my sister shared one, father and youngest
brother another. David and Bill and I shared the smallest. The
fourth room was the kitchen, livingroom, dining room,
playroom, washingroom, or whatever else you cared to call it. A
kitten had drowned in the well and so water for cooking and
drinking had to be carried in enamel pails from a spring half a
mile away. Rain water from the roof was caught in a huge cask
and used for washing. There was no electricity. Two rooms had
fireplaces. There was no means of heating the others. The most
private place was the dry lavatory outside, next to the hen-house.
So much that had been taken for granted—space, warmth, light,

hot and cold water on tap—disappeared suddenly and was missed, including the bath!

Our room was next to grandmother's and every night we could hear her praying earnestly in Gaelic, often at great length. She had ruled her own family totally until war and marriage gave independence to her children, except for my father who only achieved it late in life, after his second marriage. In her the classical struggle between nature and grace raged unceasingly. She was intelligent, strong-willed, quick tempered, often rough-tongued, and possessive. When a son married she wept. She and her daughter quarrelled early and long, according to report. They were perhaps very much alike and got on better at a distance. My mother was the only woman to preserve independence under the same roof without quarrelling with her, having a quiet unruffled dignity which could not be shaken and an ability to distinguish the important from the trivial in life which made her socially flexible.

My grandmother was a strict sabbatarian, one of the things that made our new way of life more burdensome than it might otherwise have been. She had never beaten her own children on Sunday for misdemeanours committed that day: they were punished before breakfast on Monday morning, invariably. She never forgot a promised punishment. Now my father and all of us had to go to church every Sunday. We sat for nearly two and a half hours, through an English service and then a Gaelic service, getting home for lunch at two o'clock unless the sermon was exceptionally long. There were no hymns, only metrical psalms, but sung to great tunes. The bi-annual Communion Sundays were unforgettably moving. In summer they were held in a clearing in a wood beside the church, to accommodate the influx of worshippers from other congregations. *The Lord's my shepherd*, sung to the tune *Wiltshire* on a hot fragrant summer day among the pines, brought earth and heaven together in a point. *All people that on earth do dwell* sung to the tune *Old Hundredth*, put *Onward, Christian soldiers* into a shade from which it never emerged.

In the Gaelic services we sang long psalm tunes of the kind now available on records from the School of Scottish Studies in the University of Edinburgh. A precentor gave out the psalm line by line, his solitary voice answered by a long wave of sound from the people. Little though my grasp of Gaelic was, and is, it was enough to take me along as we sang 'O m'anam beannaich fhein a nis, Beannaich Iehobha mor.' During the Gaelic sermon the mind roamed happily as the invariable pandrops and peppermints melted slowly in the mouth, but occasionally the rise and fall of a preacher's voice held one's ear with its beauty.

The little church in Kilmorack was served from Dingwall. The minister was a kindly man who was said to have suffered much. He was eloquent in Gaelic or English and spoke with sincerity. I remember consciously nothing of his preaching except that he loved the prophet Isaiah and must have reached other hearts when he spoke of God's mercy towards a sinful people, taking some such text as *Isaiah* 54:8: 'In a moment of indignation have I hid my face a little while from thee, but with everlasting kindness have I had mercy on thee, said the Lord, the Redeemer.' When he preached on the Passion of Christ he was carried away, and I with him. He preached once a year on the perils of Romanism, as he was obliged to do by higher authority in the Free Presbyterian Church; what he said seemed to apply mainly to Spaniards, Italians, and Irish, a poor ignorant and feckless sort of people anyway. The Roman Catholics we knew were different, being decent people and good neighbours whose services were even shorter than those of the Church of Scotland, and attended probably more out of loyalty to ancestors than for any deeper reason, since they were so short! It was important not to take our good neighbours as typical of Romanism. They were decent Highland people who did not try to pervert other people's religion. The real menace lay in Glasgow and the 'Glasgow Irish', and in London where, we were told, no less than ninety-six per cent of Fleet Street was Romanist.

At that time only three Catholics had made any impression on my life. The first was 'Ferret', a boarded-out Glasgow boy of about my own age, with an Irish name; thin in body, fierce in action, and with a little sharp face which explained his nickname. We met in my first term at the village school because although he went to the Catholic school we travelled for half a mile on the same road. One afternoon I was walking slowly home, studying *The Shorter Catechism* in readiness for next morning's religious lesson, when he came up silently behind me. He looked at my hand. 'What's that yer readin?' I showed him. 'Huh! That's no a right catechism. Here!' He pulled a grubby crushed booklet from his trouser pocket, opened it and stuck a dirty nail-bitten finger on the words 'Thou art Peter, and upon this rock I will build my church.' He sounded in earnest when he added 'See! Your church is no' the right one!' We were already at his gate, to my relief. 'Ferret' and religion had never connected before in my mind and to have him quoting the Bible with such an appearance of conviction was disturbing. However, we never talked about religion again and he was soon moved to some other foster home.

The second Catholic was our immediate neighbour in the village. Miss Fraser was a large woman who suffered from goitre, the effects of which showed only too plainly. She attended Mass every morning and went to the chapel to pray every evening after her day's work as a book-keeper in one of the village shops. On Friday evenings she made the Stations of the Cross, using a little book of prayers which I saw one day. It had pictures of Jesus being scourged, crowned with thorns, carrying the cross, hanging on it, and then being taken down from it. The prayers were strange to me then, but they did not seem to belong to Antichrist. 'I love Thee, my Jesus, my love above all things. I repent with my whole heart of having offended Thee. Never permit me to separate myself from Thee again. Grant that I may love Thee always, and then do with me what Thou wilt. Jesus, for love of me Thou goest to Calvary. Grant that I may live, suffer, and die with Thee.' Miss Fraser nursed her old bed-ridden father at home for years, until he died. Then she fostered a Glasgow family of two sisters and a brother, Katherine, Mary and James. Kathy was a year or so older than I, a thoughtful, warm-hearted girl who was a greater help when my mother died than anyone else around. She talked about death with more ease than most grown-ups and with a calm assurance of the Resurrection.

During my mother's first illness Miss Fraser came in every morning for a time and got our breakfast ready. She and my mother were good friends. She and my father had known each other since childhood. He seemed always a little wary of her. She had a quick wit and loved verbal fencing. We children thought her great fun, especially when she played ghosts with us until the house thrilled with shrieks and laughter. Her own house was crowded with herself and three children in three rooms which were packed with furniture, pictures and statues. In the

living room there was a crucifix, a picture of the Virgin Mary
with a little shelf beneath it on which a light burned day and
night, a picture of Jesus pointing to a heart surrounded by rays,
and a big framed engraving of Mary, Queen of Scots, going to
execution. I seem to remember another engraving showing the
meeting of Prince Charlie and Lochiel, but although Miss Fraser
revered Queen Mary as a martyr she shared my father's attitude
towards the prince, for whom they had very little regard.

The third Catholic was another neighbour, Granny
Macgregor, an old widow from one of the traditional Catholic
areas in the east of Scotland. She was incredibly like my own
grandmother, not least in her Sunday observance. It was a
surprise to learn that she also read her Bible every day and I
was curious to see what it was like. Miss Fraser showed me her
own copy which, as far as I could see, was much the same as
mine except that it had an extra number of books in it. Catholics
had Bibles after all and it was only the Old Testament which
had books that were not in the King James version. The New
Testament seemed almost the same as ours; it certainly had no
extra books. I saw that the Beatitudes, in Matthew chapter 5,
had a few words which were different, but the sense was the
same. It did not strike me then that there might possibly be
some significance in the Catholic use of 'justice' instead of the
Protestant 'righteousness' in verse 10: 'Blessed are they that
suffer persecution for Justice's sake; for theirs is the kingdom of
heaven.'

At that particular stage, however, comparison of texts was less
absorbing than the study of the two old ladies whose religious
character appeared so much alike although one was a Free
Presbyterian and the other a Roman Catholic. They even looked
alike at times, especially on their way to church in black coats
and bonnets. Everyone who knew them agreed that they were
'strict' and that was certainly true of the one with whom I was
daily involved. The problems of living in my grandmother's
house dominated everything for a time and made careful study
of that old lady an urgent necessity.

7

It vexed my grandmother that she was not as fit as she would have liked to be. There was so much to do which once would have been simple but now strained the resources of a seventy-five-year-old body. In addition privacy and quiet had gone for ever. She was caught up in the tensions of an unhappy son and five vigorous young children who were a greater burden than she had anticipated, since their father was unable to shoulder much of the responsibility which was rightly his. He left us to ourselves for what appeared a very long time after my mother's death, emerging from his withdrawn state only when we were noisy. It was made clear by my grandmother that what my father would not or could not do I, as the eldest son, would have to tackle as far as I was able. This was accepted by my father inasmuch as he expected me to look after the younger ones, which meant keeping them occupied so that he was not disturbed and they did not get into trouble.

There was much to do. In principle each of us was expected to help with the daily chores. The smallest, for example, could at least carry in kindling for the fire. There was wood to be sawn and chopped, coal to be brought in, water to be carried from the well, and vegetables from the garden. The hens had to be fed and their shed cleaned out once a week. The earth closet had to be kept wholesome, which meant emptying its contents each Saturday into a hole dug for that purpose in the midden and then scrubbing and disinfecting seat and floor with a strong solution of lysol. In the house itself floors had to be swept and scrubbed, the fireplace polished with Brasso and black lead, the kitchen table and chairs scrubbed each week; and daily there were dishes to wash.

At the weekend unwashed dishes accumulated. All work not strictly necessary stopped after we had polished our boots and shoes on Saturday evening. Most of Sunday's food was cooked or at least prepared on Saturday, ready to heat up on Sunday. The Sunday breakfast of bacon and egg was the exception to this rule and there was no embargo on making tea three or four times during the day. The main Sunday meal always consisted

of broth or lentil soup, cold beef or mutton with boiled potatoes
and cabbage or turnip, followed by a milk pudding. There were
four varieties of milk pudding, rice, semolina, sago and tapioca.
The pots and dishes gathered, to be washed by my sister and
myself at 6.30 on Monday morning, supported by biscuits with
tea which we made and enjoyed while the washing-up water was
being heated. There was marvellous peace and quiet on those
Monday mornings when everyone else was still in bed. We were
not sleepy, because everyone had gone to bed early the night
before to shorten the boredom of Sunday. In fine summer
weather Jan and I were often up soon after five o'clock to enjoy
the fresh morning and the song of thrush and blackbird in the
garden. Usually we made the porridge for the family's breakfast
and about 7.15 took a cup of tea to Granny in bed.

Sunday was difficult. The morning was of course taken up
with breakfast and church. As my grandmother hated missing
church my father found no escape from driving the family there,
except when he could plead sickness, which was rarely.
Consequently I could count on being left at home at least every
second Sunday, alone for nearly four hours with nothing to do
except the small preparation for Sunday dinner. My
grandmother would have been horrified had she known what
use was often made of these hours, which were not spent with
the two texts permitted for Sunday reading, the Bible and
Bunyan's *Pilgrim's Progress* but rather with the Harmsworth
History of the World or sundry faintly pornographic magazines,
mild by today's standards but sufficiently stimulating to a
thirteen or fourteen-year-old boy with a lively imagination.

After our meal my father retired to his room where he read a
batch of Sunday papers smuggled in by a friendly neighbour. At
three o'clock I was expected to lead an hour of catechism and
Bible study, under the matriarchal eye if I was lucky; otherwise
on my own, until some disturbance of the peace brought a
wrathful adult from his or her bed to restore order. Although
the younger ones had individual wooden stools, placed so as to
keep each out of arm's reach of the others as far as possible,
quarrels could begin with a silent exchange of sneering or
contemptuous looks leading to an outburst of verbal abuse or
the swift flight of a bible through the air. My two youngest
brothers were experts in the art of subtle provocation.
Eventually, when I began to earn some money by holiday work,

I fell back on a system of examinations and prizes which reduced the tension a little, after I had recognised that everyone would have to receive a prize, if they had behaved reasonably well.

What might be called management problems were made easier for a time by something called the 'Union of Kosalrio'. Some children at school in Wick had formed a Secret Society which David and I were considered too young to join. We decided to form our own and after the move to Inverness-shire one or two special friends were admitted to membership. At first our society had no name and its sign consisted merely of 'S' and 'S' intertwined. Its first territory was simply our garden in Wick. Inverness-shire opened up exciting possibilities. We annexed a piece of land by the River Beauly, the Lovat Estates remaining ignorant and untroubled by the presence of squatters in a swampy coppice known to its invaders as the 'State of Kosalrio'. Kosalrio had a President, being intended as a republic, but some of its members showed a hankering for grandeur which made it politic to devolve power and to recognise high-sounding titles. The Prince-Emperor of Pulkostria, the Duchess of Hidomel, the Lord of Delvalern and the Duke of Warga were content to be members of a federation which allowed them to muck about as much as they liked on their own patch of riverside. If the Lord of Delvalern began to sling clay bullets at the Duke of Warga he could be brought to trial, if the Prince-Emperor and the Duchess were not too busy with other ploys. If the Prince-Emperor sat among the reeds loftily declaring that today he was Moses among the bulrushes, and coldly denying that he was merely in a huff, the other potentates could avoid his territory until he became bored and decided to join in whatever project was afoot. The Union had a unit of currency, the 'micula', in which members paid for such goods as pine cones, broom pods, lumps of mica schist or sandstone pebbles, and paid also federal taxes which would be used to finance the work of building a federal meeting-place, clearing paths, or gathering fuel for camp fires.

After our mother's death and the move from the village the first territory of Kosalrio was abandoned once more to the Lovat Estates, but there was compensation in the shape of a field which went with our grandmother's cottage, lying behind it and the garden. It was beautifully irregular, dipping from east and west to a central hollow, with broom on each piece of higher ground; and it contained a small sandpit. Behind it lay a very large sandpit in which sand-martins nested annually, and behind that stretched several acres of dense broom. The meetings of Kosalrians were held among the broom and became a mixture of the real and the fantastic at which members discussed not only the price of broom and sand but also the division of domestic chores for each week. The adults in the household knew nothing of these meetings, the explosions of anger or frustration which marked them sometimes, or the anxiety raised by a young brother's tearful threat to drown himself if life did not become happier. When the afternoon came when he ran out of the house and towards the river David and I went after him with fear in our hearts of which the grown-ups knew nothing.

The affairs of Kosalrio were recorded in its own alphabet, invented when life was easier. Just as the Kosalrian game provided an outlet for feelings, and an instrument of practical use in day-to-day affairs, so its alphabet made it possible for me not only to write down safely the decision reached at meetings but also to express bitter feelings about people and about God without fear of making the home situation worse if someone stumbled upon the notebook. God had brought us into an unhappy situation, and my father was doing wretchedly little to help. At least he had not taken to drink. The good earlier memories that the older ones among us had, enabled us to discount much of what happened now, and not to take it too seriously when he said, 'I wish none of you had ever been born!' As for God—He made trouble for everyone and had always done so if one believed the Bible. One could only hope it was true that in the end everything worked out for good, and that one day we would appreciate the love which was said to be watching over us and actually giving us strength to endure the confusion and the pain. In the meantime the *Book of Job* and the *Psalms* alike acquired new relevance, and God was addressed with a new directness and intensity, sometimes indeed with shouts directed not so much to Him as at Him.

So we struggled to keep things together, helped by our father's better days when his old spirit seemed to be returning, and by our grandmother's love and care. There were days when she was prostrate and we had to cope somehow with cooking, baking, ironing and mending, and occasionally washing clothes when no one else was available. When Granny was ill we nursed her and then she was wonderfully patient, her mind intent on recovering sufficient strength to rise, if only for one or two hours of urgent work. When confined to bed she had more time to pray, and one of us would be called to read the Bible to her now and then during the day if we were at home and always in the evening. Her faith and hope and love carried her along, and us with her, for five years until my father married again. During those years her most constant prayer became very familiar to us all: '*A Thighearna! Dean trocair orm*' – 'Lord, have mercy on me.'

8

Some weeks after my mother's death a new academic session began, the last one for me in the village school.

'What will you do when you are fourteen?' my father asked, 'leave school and find work? or do you want to continue?'

'I would like to go on,' was my answer.

'In that case' he replied, 'you'll have to find money for bus fares to the town, for books, and if possible for clothes and shoes. I can provide board and lodging, but it will be up to you to manage the rest.'

This was understandable. I suggested that if such was to be our arrangement it would only be fair that I should handle my own money, to which he agreed:

'Open a Post Office Savings Account.'

I did that soon afterwards, with money earned working at odd times on a neighbouring farm. There was reasonable hope of occasional work on farms or at the local sawmill, especially during school holidays, but it was essential to win scholarships as well and so to study with examinations in view. There was the possibility of an annual grant of £9 from the Local Education Authority and also the chance of winning a Highlands and Islands Trust bursary of £10 a year. A limited number of these became available annually, tenable for three years, and awarded on a basis of examination in four subjects, one of which had to be knowledge of the Bible and the *Shorter Catechism*. My other subjects were to be English, French and Latin, all studied in the village school along with History, Geography, General Science, Arithmetic, Algebra and Geometry over a three-year period.

School became enjoyable. It offered an escape from the stress of life at home. The teachers, all university graduates except the two infant mistresses, were able and congenial. There was a goal for which to work. Outside the play intervals, when four of us knocked a ball about with home-made shinty sticks or played football with an old can, there was little time and no money for games or parties. For the younger ones also school became, in some degree, an alternative to home. My youngest brother, trudging miserably three miles each day in winter cold and wet, was in the care of 'Clachy-Ann', the children's name for Miss MacLachlan who had been a pupil-teacher during my father's last year at school and had taught our youngest uncle. She and Miss Tuach, the senior infant teacher, had spent all their lives in the village except for two years at a Training College. They were totally part of village life, dedicated women with a sense of God-given vocation and well endowed with commonsense and humour. Miss MacLachlan reminded me of one of Granny's big brown hens as she moved imperturbably along the short stretch of road which linked her home, the school, and the church which she attended twice on Sunday. Miss Tuach was smaller and quick, with a wall eye which it was hard not to stare at, and she could become quite angry at times. Both lived to be over eighty, Miss Tuach fading away contentedly in her eighty-sixth year, having corresponded faithfully for over twenty years with my second brother, Bill, until his death after more than that number of years of difficult but eventful illness. By an unexpected conjunction of events I was back in the village on the day of her funeral in time to join, in a packed church, some of the hundreds of others who loved her.

David's favourite teacher was Miss Shaw, who seemed to know by instinct what you were feeling and showed understanding in a silent glance or smile. My favourite was Miss Mackenzie, who taught the last class in the school's primary section. She was short and trim, with a swing in her walk; a study in black and white with dark hair and pale complexion, black skirt and white blouse. Her eyes rested on everyone without favouritism but sometimes she seemed to speak directly to you, as one day when she was explaining the word 'philosopher'—'a lover of wisdom, which is what we should all try to be,' and she looked at me as she spoke, or so it seemed. There was another occasion, significant at the time but somehow impossible to explain then to other people. The class had been given a poem by John Drinkwater to learn by heart over the weekend. On Monday morning child after child stood up miserably and recited a mangled half-learned verse. Miss Mackenzie began to look angry and more and more nervous tension began to build up in the class. My turn came. I had enjoyed learning the poem, but now my stomach was knotted and I could only remember the first line. I plunged into it, and the class faded away. I saw only the toll-house about which the poet spoke, and felt his words. Then there was silence; the class was staring, at me, at Miss Mackenzie. She said quietly 'Ten out of ten.' There was a little rustle as I sat down, the other children relaxed, and I was called upon no more that morning.

Life in the senior section of the village school began not quite so happily, in some respects. There was a headmaster I did not like, and he did not like me. He taught Latin, which became a nightmare subject as arithmetic had been years before, and my parents decided that I must give it up. It was a relief when he left after my first term among the seniors, to become a school inspector. The new headmaster was a Free Presbyterian and known therefore to my father and grandmother. I resumed the study of Latin with him, for half-an-hour daily after the usual school hours until I had caught up with the rest of the Latin class. He was a burly man with a toothbrush moustache and a red face, bursting with frustrated energy which was poured into the school as far as it was possible. He had been an artillery captain during the war and twice weekly the older boys, aged between eleven and fourteen were given infantry drill as a form of physical education. It would, he believed, smarten us up. The first class taken by him each morning began with the singing of a psalm and the recitation of the Lord's Prayer. We were introduced to a wide range of old Scottish psalm tunes, and the Bible reading which constituted religious education— supplemented by memorising the *Shorter Catechism*—was directed by him with gusto. There was something disturbing about him, a smell of violence close to the surface. Three occasions stay in my memory. One morning he intercepted a drawing passed between two girls which revealed their curiosity about his sexual endowment. Corporal punishment was not unusual and as a rule caused no great concern, but the ferocity with which these two thirteen-year-old girls were belted three times on each hand sickened me even then. It was strange too to hear a grown man shout to a boy, 'You'll remember it, Fraser, if you get my knee on your chest,' and I hated him when he threw a quiet, backward, orphan cousin of mine against a blackboard so violently that boy and blackboard fell in a heap on the floor. Yet my brother David was devoted to him and received, as I did, steady encouragement from him.

Nastiness was not all on one side. There was thoughtless persecution of a highly-strung teacher by the senior class. He was a little jerky man, tense and unsure of himself before a block of somewhat uninterested children which included several boys much bigger than himself who were counting the months to leaving. If he tried to strap one of them the offender's hand would be quickly withdrawn before the belt made contact. On at least one occasion it was grabbed and held while he tugged at it futilely. These humiliations were mild compared to the humming torment which was invented in the same class. While he wrote something on the blackboard a faint hum would begin, and stop as he looked round, only to begin again as he resumed writing. Invariably he asked who was responsible, to be faced with a staring silence. When he moved suspiciously towards one section of the class the humming would start behind him. The object was to work him into a frenzy of helpless anger, when he would rush from one part of the class to another, trying to identify his persecutors and visibly close to tears. He held a good degree and could explain things clearly. It was plain to us that the headmaster despised him, and before long he left to teach smaller children in a primary school where his specialised knowledge of science would not be required.

Work went well, except in mathematics. I wrote verse, some of which Uncle Tom sent to *The Weekly Scotsman*, which printed it in the 'Children's Corner' and sent in return each time a book of some sort, one being a lucid introduction to rhyme and metre whose title and author I have forgotten. I began to read H. G. Wells, Edgar Rice Burroughs' *Tarzan* stories and his tales of Mars and possible life on other planets, Edgar Wallace, Rider Haggard, Zane Gray's 'westerns', and stories of adventure and of boarding school life borrowed from a friend at school. These were the light entertainment sandwiched

between domestic crises and work of one kind or another. I was
tired of Scott and Dickens and Alexandre Dumas, and even more
weary of John Bunyan and the Bible.

The examination for the Highlands and Islands Bursary
Competition came at last; a room filled mostly with complete
strangers, an old respectable gentleman sitting behind a
newspaper as invigilator. The examination papers were
straightforward, but an unforeseen problem arose during the
religious paper. Lifting my head for a moment, while I thought
out some point, I saw a boy with a *Shorter Catechism* under the
desk, obviously copying an answer which he did not know. For
a moment I panicked. A bursary was essential if I was to remain
at school, but how could I win if there was cheating? Should I
draw attention to him? Perhaps he needed a bursary desperately
also. All candidates came from poor or relatively poor families.
He could hardly copy much at the rate he was going. He couldn't
know his stuff anyway if he had to rely on cheating. I got on
with my own writing and gave him no further attention. When
the results were published I had won a Junior Bursary of £10 a
year and knew that in due course I might hope for a senior award
of £20 a year if I qualified for entrance to a university. My
father was pleased, the teachers and all the family, but decorously
reserved in expressing their pleasure. With a minimum of £19 a
year guaranteed for three years I could look forward to entering
Inverness Royal Academy at the age of fourteen, one of a
minority from country schools to attend that ancient foundation
which claimed an unbroken history from the time, about 1233,
when a group of Dominican Friars settled in Inverness.

9

The move of little fish to bigger pools can be exciting and
exhilarating. The town of Inverness in 1931 with a population
of 23,000 dwarfed the village, with its 802 inhabitants. The
Academy had over 760 pupils; the village school, with about 230,

was almost exactly the size of the Academy's primary section. At first the surge of bodies through the centrally placed assembly hall and up or down stairs every time a bell rang was bewildering; it was easy to land red-faced in the wrong classroom. The classroom plan of the Academy became clear after a few days, as did other things previously unexpected. For example, only Fifth or Sixth Form members lounged against certain radiators, boys and girls gathered on opposite sides of the assembly hall during intervals. The school day began at nine o'clock and ended on some days at 3.30 pm, at 4.15 on others. There was a bus to be caught every morning at eight. The journey took about 45 minutes. There were afternoon buses for the return journey at four and five o'clock. Most of us from the country carried sandwiches for lunch, as some had done at the village school, and we had our main meal of the day when home again in the evening.

The Rector wore a gown, as did the Second Master and the Lady Superintendent who supervised the girls' behaviour. Each new pupil was interviewed by the Rector, an Englishman with a science degree from an English university. He frowned on hearing that I wished to learn Greek. 'Do you intend to become a minister?' 'Oh, no!' I answered cheerfully, 'but I like what I've read in translation and want to know more.' He objected that in the Academy pupils began Greek in their third year and brushed aside the suggestion that I might catch up with the other fourth year pupils, a small class of three. 'There is enough available in translation. You will have to follow a science course. H'm, mathematics weak I see. In that case it had better be Chemistry with Botany rather than Physics.' So it was settled for the next two years. Botany was a substitute for Biology, which was not on the curriculum. The master responsible for it was an able botanist, an indifferent chemist, and an unenthusiastic but adequate teacher. We got on well after an early difference about a plant specimen which I brought in one Monday morning. After a cursory glance he dismissed it contemptuously as a poor specimen of Shepherd's Purse. 'But it's Teesdalia!' I protested. 'Rubbish, boy! Teesdalia isn't found in the Highlands;' but he picked it up, and after close examination agreed as to its identity while still dubious about my description of where I had found it. In the end he agreed to travel out to meet me on the next Saturday afternoon so that he might view the plant actually growing in unlikely surroundings. Having seen it for himself he suggested that seed might have been carried by chance on a railway wagon from Teesdale to Ross-shire, blowing from the wagon on to the embankment on which the plant now grew. Having no better explanation to offer each other we settled for that and shared from that day an interest in ecology. Had he been as ardent a teacher as he was a botanist my life might have taken a different course and botany have become more than a hobby for which I am grateful.

The ardent teachers were in other departments, in language and literature, history and mathematics. The senior mathematics master proved his point that there was no inherent reason for my poor showing in his subject, having challenged me successfully to give as much attention to it for one term as I gave usually to English literature. After that term I continued shamelessly on my way, unabashed by six per cent in a trigonometry exam and waging public debate in favour of poetry as against mathematics with an obstinacy only partly explained by the excitement of discovering new fields in literature and a growing facility in verse-making. Home had given me a wider experience of poetry than was offered in school, where 'The boy stood on the burning deck', 'Lord Ullin's Daughter', and 'Daffodils', were examples of dominant poetic species. Now there were enthusiasts who knew more than anyone I had ever met, more even than Uncle Tom and my father, although the former had known a flock of Georgian poets when they were all young in London, and had met W. B. Yeats in the flesh. I was ready for Methuen's anthology of modern English lyrics, for Masefield, Blunden, de la Mare and the early Yeats, Flecker, Housman and W. H. Davies, but not so well prepared for the head English teacher, D. J. Macdonald, rendering Chaucer and Milton in a mellow West Highland voice. The leap was great from Wordsworth's daffodils to his 'Ode to the Intimations of Immortality', or even from Shakespeare's *Julius Caesar* and *Macbeth* to *King Lear* and *Hamlet*. As great in another way was the leap from Caesar's *Gallic Wars* to the epic poetry of Vergil. I can never forget the morning when we received our copies of *Aeneid*, Books I and II, and listened to the senior classics teacher, Alexander Duthie, reading:

Arma virumque cano, Troiae qui primus ab oris

Italiam fato profugus Lavinaque venit;

and I was glad that I had persevered with Latin. 'Pa' Duthie, small in build, but great in personality, had degrees in classics and in philosophy from St Andrews University; literature, in his mind, was never detached from the people and the culture in which it had been made. He and 'D. J.' led us not simply to texts, but to people whose thoughts and feelings became more vivid and immediate as they read and commented on their work. Both encouraged us to write; blank verse, sonnets, ballads, triolets, Latin hexameters and elegiac couplets. Horizons continued to expand as the way was pointed to other literatures, to Scandinavian, Gaelic, Italian, Spanish, and French—over which last there was disagreement, since Mr Duthie denied the existence of any French verse worthy to be called poetry.

That was probably one reason for the lack of cordiality between him and the Lady Superintendent, who was also head of the modern languages department and taught French; a strange lady, with marked social prejudices. 'Your family is quite poor, isn't it?' she asked me one day as we stood on the balcony outside her room, looking down into the assembly hall and waiting for a bell. To my affirmative she replied, 'Well, then, how do you come to have such good manners?' The bell rang as I hesitated over my reply. Manners had to do with respect for people and were not the same thing, my parents had pointed out, as social conventions. 'Any fool can learn what to do with knives and forks,' my father had said once, 'but that's not the same thing as good manners.' At that time I had not heard the praise of my grandfather spoken by old men nearly forty years later: 'One of the rare few, nature's gentlemen.' Nor had I heard the story of how a sportsman for whom my grandfather had sometimes worked, travelled specially from London to attend his funeral, walking hat in hand for three miles behind the hearse. My family had never mentioned that. So I looked at the Lady Superintendent and with a slight shrug said, 'I don't know. That's how we were brought up!' Later, on the homeward bus, I reflected on the contrast between her abrupt and angular manner and the graciousness which had seemed so natural in my mother and which appeared to come so easily even to my tough and usually outspoken grandmother when she greeted strangers or guests. There was no other occasion, as far as I remember, when social snobbery surfaced in school life. It must be added in justice to the Lady Superintendent that she taught French highly efficiently, and introduced us to Giraudoux's *Amphitryon 38* when that play was scarcely known to our contemporaries in France, and in fact little appreciated by us.

At the Academy, each year was divided into three streams, A, B and C. Pupils studying Art, or Domestic Science, or Commercial Subjects, were in C as a matter of course. Division between A and B streams depended on ability, and it was possible for someone in a B stream to join an A stream for a subject in which he or she was particularly good, although that did not happen very often. All those in an A stream were regarded as potential university candidates; some of those in a B stream might be in that category, but as exceptions to the average in their stream. There was no attempt to push any of us towards university if we had other plans for the future, as several already had as early as their fourth year.

Debate was encouraged in the English department and was a regular Friday afternoon activity. In addition to thrashing ancient themes such as 'town versus country' we tackled various contemporary issues. The League of Nations was still in being and I was labelled pessimist for holding that its end was in sight, when it failed to prevent the Japanese invasion of Jehol. Pacifism began to seem not only inseparable from an attempt to follow Christ but the only alternative to even more disastrous wars than that of 1914–18. There was little concern with political parties in our debates but passionate argument about education and questions of war and peace. There was a stout girl from the Outer Isles, Effie Morrison, who was an able debater, and she and I carried on long epistolary arguments throughout school holidays, in sixteen to twenty page letters which always began 'Dear Mr Ross' and 'Dear Miss Morrison' and concluded 'Yours sincerely'. More formidable in debate than the boys, the girls were a remarkable group: Ena, Alice, Frances, Lilian, Sheila, Anella, and Jessamy, able to hold their own in any company, or so at least it appeared at the time. Male chauvinism had no chance of impressing them but it was not much in evidence anyway, even when we debated the motion 'That woman's place is in the home'. We had been used to co-education all our lives and, apart from a few from remote areas who boarded at the boys' hostel or the girls' hostel, we lived at home with brothers and sisters. It was a boy from an English boarding school who came at the age of sixteen, lost his head and 'seduced' an orphan girl from the country. The event was hardly noticed. Only those of us who lived in the same district were aware of her pregnancy and we did not mention it elsewhere. It is doubtful if any of the staff knew about it as she was old enough to leave school at any time she chose and simply gave notice that she would not be coming back after one vacation. Her friends saw her, of course, as a victim of English education! The English boy, now friendless, left after one year in Inverness.

Domestic responsibilities, distance, and shortage of money detached me from extra-curricular activities such as the annual school dance, the play, the annual picnic, the school camp, or any part in sports. It was possible however to become involved with the 'school magazine', a lively production which combined gossip and artistic ambition in varying proportions. and occasionally I went home to tea with Jessamy, or with Alastair Duthie, who were both in my year. My chief activity in Inverness outside school hours was browsing in Mackay's bookshop in the High Street or at the second-hand bookstall in the Market. The latter was tantalising; it was impossible to buy books there as Dad would have thrown out any of its worn volumes as a likely source of infection, but Mackay's Bookshop held large stocks of Oxford 'World Classics' and Dent's 'Everyman's Library' which sometimes made me late for the 4 o'clock bus. It was not possible to buy much, but over the first two years at the Academy I bought my first volume of Icelandic sagas, Snorri Sturlason's *Heimskringla*, Thomas à Kempis's *Imitation of Christ*, the *Koran*, the *Old Testament Apocrypha* and the *Little Flowers of St Francis*. A Japanese pen-friend wrote enthusiastically about a novel called *Ulysses*, the work of an Irishman called Joyce, but Homer's *Ulysses* was the only one known to Mackay's or indeed to anyone in the Academy, and my knowledge of modern novels rested with Wells and Kipling, although Thomas Hardy was suggested for further reading when we were in the sixth year.

We knew little of Scottish literature apart from some ballads, such as 'Sir Patrick Spens', 'The Battle of Otterburn', and 'Thomas the Rhymer'; some poems by Burns, Lady Nairne's Jacobite songs, and Sir Walter Scott's narrative poems, particularly 'The Lady of the Lake' and 'Marmion'. Of his novels, *The Heart of Midlothian*, *Old Mortality*, *Waverley* and *Rob Roy* were studied in one year or another. Stevenson's *Kidnapped* and *The Master of Ballantrae* were other set texts. The school library or the town library made available books by Neil Munro, D. K. Broster, John Buchan, James Barrie, J. J. Bell, and Neil Gunn. My father had known Gunn's family for a time when living in Caithness, and our own boyhood experience strengthened the appeal of *Morning Tide* as a book close to the reality of the Highlands. We knew nothing of the harsher life shown in *The House with the Green Shutters* or in Lewis Grassic Gibbon's *A Scots Quair*, whose three volumes were published during my years at the Academy and so had not yet had time to become classics. Our 'modern' Scottish poets were Charles Murray, Violet Jacob and Marion Angus. In my primary school days I had starred at Sunday School soirees by reciting:

The bairnies cuddle doon at nicht
Wi' muckle faucht an' din.
'Oh, try an' sleep, ye waukrife rogues!
Yer faither's comin' in;'

while an audience recently anglicised marvelled, 'How he gets his tongue round the words!' Had I continued public recitation the Scots poem of my choice at this later stage would doubtless have been Murray's 'The Whistle':

He cut a sappy sucker from the muckle rodden tree,
He trimmed it, an' he wet it, an' he thumped it on his knee;
He never heard the teuchat when the harrow broke her eggs,
He missed the craggit heron nabbin' puddocks in the seggs,
He forgot to hound the collie at the cattle when they strayed,
But you should hae seen the whistle that the wee herd made!

Scottish verse held little interest compared to Palgrave's *Golden Treasury*. I knew little Gaelic and less Scots; a vast body of English and Latin literature demanded more time than was available for its exploration and Palgrave was a constant companion on bus journeys throughout my first year in

Inverness. My adolescent mood was suited by Vergil's '*Sunt lacrimae rerum et mentem mortalia tangunt*' and a year later by lines from Horace's ode '*Eheu, fugaces! Postume, Postume, Labuntur anni*'. I learned by heart not Murray's lines, but such verses from Palgrave as Shirley's 'Death the Leveller':

> The glories of our blood and state
> Are shadows, not substantial things.
> There is no armour against fate,
> Death lays his icy hand on kings.
> Sceptre and crown must tumble down,
> And in the dust be equal made
> With the poor crooked scythe and spade.

Fitzgerald's rendering of *The Rubaiyat of Omar Khayyam* caught my attention for the first time, and Flecker's *Golden Journey* to Samarkand:

> We are the Pilgrims, master; we shall go
> Always a little further: it may be
> Beyond that last blue mountain barred with snow,
> Across that angry or that glimmering sea;
> White on a throne or guarded in a cave,
> There lives a prophet who can understand
> Why men were born: but surely we are brave
> Who make the Golden Journey to Samarkand.

At fifteen I believed I was on a journey, *that* at least, but greatly uncertain as to an exact destination.

It was somewhere in my first or second year at the Academy that I had a significant dream. In Wick, when about seven and eight years old, I had a frequently recurring dream in which I was walking along the street, most often on the bridge across the river, when a great engine came roaring down threateningly towards me. Always at the last moment the driver and I saw each other as friends and I was swung up into the cab, safe and sound beside him. That dream was succeeded by another after we left Wick for Beauly. In the new dream I explored a strange building, part farm part house, in which there were lofts and attics stretching one after another, interesting but sometimes menacing, to be crept through very quietly and carefully. Through slits in the planking it was sometimes possible to see who came and went, and whether or not they were friends. The third dream came only once. I stood by a broad river, alone. As I looked upstream a boat appeared in the far distance and held my attention as it drew steadily nearer. It was full of people, and among them I saw my mother. Immediately I moved forward, eager to go aboard and join her. She smiled and shook her head, pointing downstream as the boat drew level with where I was. I followed her signal and saw, far off, a great blaze of golden light towards which the boat and its company sailed on; and I knew that I had to wait for another boat, but felt at peace.

10

My father made no comment on the books I bought, but two of them had an unforeseen effect on my grandmother and myself. It had become customary for me to read a chapter of the Bible to her, in Gaelic, each night after she had gone to bed. There were frequent interruptions as she corrected my pronunciation, and it is doubtful if my bad reading did more than refresh her memory of passages which she already knew almost by heart. One evening, tired of stumbling through the Gaelic text of the *Book of Kings*, I followed it with a chapter in English, from the first book of the *Imitation of Christ*. She listened closely with obvious approval, and selections from Thomas à Kempis became a fairly frequent part of the evening reading. All that she knew about him was that he had lived before the Reformation. She showed no curiosity about his history; it was enough that his book showed him to be a 'man of God'. Encouraged by her reception of *The Imitation* I mentioned that I had a book of Jewish religious writings which were not part of the Bible, but worth reading, and so passages from *Wisdom* and *Ecclesiasticus* came into our programme. At first I was simply pleased that it was proving possible to diversify the evening readings, but soon I began to reflect on the ease with which she accepted the writings of a medieval Catholic and some Hellenised pre-Christian Jews as food for her soul.

Her acceptance of à Kempis came from a shared sense of sin and of the transitory nature of this world, the world which she nevertheless enjoyed so richly in many ways. Passages such as the following perfectly agreed with her own belief and experience:

> Turn to the Lord with your whole heart, and forsake this wretched world: your soul shall find rest.
>
> The kingdom of God is peace and Joy in the Holy Ghost.
>
> Christ will come to you and discover his consolation to you, if you prepare him a worthy dwelling within you.
>
> All his glory and beauty are from within, and there it is that he takes his delight.
>
> Many are his visits to the man of inward life. With such a one he holds delightful converse, granting him sweet comfort, much peace, and an intimacy astonishing beyond measure.
>
> Come then, faithful soul, prepare your heart for this your spouse, so that he may vouchsafe to come to you and dwell within you.
>
> For so he says: 'If any man love me, he will keep my word, and we will come to him and make our dwelling with him.'
>
> Make room therefore for Christ, and refuse entrance to all others.
>
> When you have Christ, you are rich and have need of naught else.
>
> He will provide for you, and be in all things your faithful procurator; you shall not need to look to men.
>
> Put your whole trust in God; let him be your fear and your love.
>
> He will answer for you, and will graciously do for you as shall be best.
>
> You have no lasting city here. Wherever you may be, you are a stranger and a pilgrim, nor will you ever have rest, except you be inwardly united with Christ.
>
> (*Imitation*, Bk. 2:1, 1–6)

Although she longed to receive Communion she never ventured to do so. The custom in the Free Presbyterian Church and the Free Church of 'fencing the tables' was too much for her. As

the minister read out the awful list of sins and shortcomings
which were held to debar people from approaching the Lord's
Table, and the even more awesome list of virtues which might
qualify someone to approach, she judged herself invariably to be
utterly unworthy and sat still in her pew, head bent and tearful,
while those who felt sure of their predestination to eternal glory
went forward. I did not read to her the passages of à Kempis
about Communion, which were strange to me at the time and
seemed better left aside, and since we had no Gaelic version she
could not read them for herself.

The *Apocrypha* presented questions which I noticed with light
interest and certainly without anxiety. Here were writings, some
of which at least sounded so like books from the Bible that one
wondered why they were not included in it. Who had decided
that they were not authentic Scripture? The Holy Spirit,
according to the minister. But how? Through the Church
apparently, which could distinguish inspired Scripture from
merely devotional writing. But if the *Apocrypha* had been
accepted as Scripture once, but was accepted as such no longer
– though half-accepted apparently by the Church of England – it
was plain that Christians had experienced great difficulty in
deciding what was and what wasn't the inspired Word of God.
Why had the Protestant churches rejected what earlier Christians
had accepted for so long? Had the *Book of Maccabees* been
rejected in fact because it advocated prayers for the dead? If *it*
was Scripture then the Roman Catholics were justified in
praying for the souls of the dead. 'It is best to leave such
questions to wiser heads' said Aunt Jess in Glenurquhart, and I
was content to do so, being caught up in school work and the
problem of how to maintain justice and peace at home.
Theoretical problems one noted and passed by, being fully
absorbed in the problems of daily living, which seemed to grow
greater as we children grew older.

Glenurquhart, of steep hillsides and hazel thickets, became a
place of occasional refuge during school holidays. There were
three 'aunts' there, strictly speaking all first cousins of my father,
on his mother's side, and all staunch members of the Free
Kirk—in other words 'Wee Frees'. Aunt Kate and her husband
Neil, and their two children, Margaret and Ian, shared a house
on the hillside above Milton of Drumnadrochit with Aunt Jess.
Aunt Maggie brought up four orphaned nephews and a niece in

a house in the tiny village of Milton. Both houses had a croft
attached; one a strip of land stretching down to the river and
sometimes flooded, the other so steep on the hill that care had to
be taken not to push the soil off it when hoeing turnips. The
four Fraser boys, my Milton cousins, were all older than me,
the youngest by a few years, Gaelic speakers and good singers.
Sometimes I stayed with them, helping on the croft, making
hay or thinning turnips, fishing on a nearby loch, poaching
rabbits on the hillside with a ferret. More often I stayed with
Aunt Kate and Uncle Neil, who surpassed even the others in
kindness and understanding. There was a little room off the
stairs and under the roof, lit only by a skylight over which the
birches leaned from the hill slope rising sweetly behind the
house. On wet days in early summer the scent of birch leaves
filled the room through the open skylight, to overflow the joy of
having a bed and a place to oneself for a few days; a place where
one could read undisturbed or simply lie and gaze up at the
flicker of light and shade among the leaves. There were
opportunities of talking to Aunt Kate, who was a good listener;
you felt all her attention was with you, and she did not deny my
account of life at home, nor brush it aside lightly. When I was
bitter because my father had struck me heavily in one of his
sudden unreasoning outbursts of rage she neither condemned
nor excused him beyond saying, 'people do cruel and unjust
things, especially when they are unhappy and worried, as your
Dad has been ever since your mother was taken'. Granny had
said, 'it is written in the fourth commandment: "Honour thy
father and thy mother"',' to which my brother Bill had retorted,
'It is also written: "Fathers provoke not your children to anger,
lest they be discouraged".' Aunt Kate said little, but her
normally tranquil face would sometimes look sad as she listened;
it was good to be in the company of her and Uncle Neil, with
his gentle, humorous outlook and his skill as a gardener. Unlike
some other friends or relations they never pried into details of
our life at home, nor spoke sarcastically about Dad or Granny.
Aunt Kate gave me a feeling that she saw beyond what was
immediately around us, as did in a lesser way the other two
aunts; there was peace about her, and in church or during family
prayers she had the same absorbed and serene appearance that I
remembered in my mother. I never heard her or Uncle Neil
speak harshly of anyone or show any interest in religious

controversy. They were products of the spiritual tradition described briefly earlier in these pages, and lived in it fully and faithfully.

Aunt Jess and Aunt Margaret appeared to be sterner stuff than their sister. The former was a big, stately woman, with a strong respect for reason and discipline. She seemed to tower from the floor in her full-length skirt. 'Better make less noise!' Uncle Neil would say with a twinkle, when my young cousins and I were romping in the house, 'or Big Jess will come through to you!' But when we hoed turnips together she was good company, and after one of our turnip field conversations she gave me Prothero on the Psalms to read, my first and helpful introduction to a commentary on Scripture. Aunt Maggie was smaller and brisker than her sisters, lively and quick-eyed, as she needed to be with a handful of boys to bring up. It seemed odd at first that she had a slight moustache, although a bearded lady had featured in one of the comic papers which we read surreptitiously at home, but plainly it did not worry her or any of the family, and I soon forgot about it. All three aunts were excellent cooks and housekeepers, with the ability to keep a house clean and bright and at the same time comfortable and homely. There was much love in Glenurquhart and I could get there by walking twelve miles through the hills. My father and grandmother must have understood my needs better than I realised at the time since they did not oppose my eager trips to the Glen.

Nearer home there was the Kate who had seen the black dog and who came to wash our sheets and blankets. Her cottage was reached in a few minutes and there I could cry or rage, while she listened with troubled eyes and occasional sympathetic noises until she judged the moment had come to make tea and bring out scones or biscuits. Her grown-up son was like Aunt Kate in his attitude to my father and myself, and became a good friend to us both. Her little girl, younger than me by some years, was often desperately ill with asthma; there was no ground to be sorry for myself when she was choking and gasping helplessly. Some people who had not seen her except when she was well and cheerful used to say it was 'all put on'. She died young. How I detested people who said 'Childhood is the happiest time in your life!'

While school and the Glenurquhart family were helping me to cope at home my younger brothers and our sister were having their own particular problems, over and above those we all shared. As the time approached for him to leave the village school one of the boys was caught in one of those bureaucratic nets in which so often children, and not only adults, are victimised. He had looked forward to securing a grant to go to the Academy in Inverness, as I had done. The village school which the family attended was in the county of Inverness; our grandmother's cottage and the neighbouring clachan were in the village postal district; so it came as a considerable shock to be told that as the cottage was two hundred yards across the county boundary into Ross-shire, he was not eligible for an Inverness-shire grant. As he had never attended a Ross-shire school, that county disclaimed any responsibility for his further education. The headmaster fought his case with vigour and Ross-shire agreed at last to give him a grant, on condition that he went to Dingwall Academy. Always loyal to his friends -- who were going to Inverness – and weary of the arguments about him, and the tensions at home, my brother left the village school as soon as he was legally free to do so, carrying with him its highest academic awards.

Bureaucracy had second thoughts when the time came for Jan to leave the local school and she was allowed to go to the Royal Academy on her grant, arriving there the term after I had left. Life at home was very hard on her. I as the eldest in the family and she as a girl were expected to shoulder more work and responsibility than our three brothers. After our mother's death no one bothered much about her appearance. She no longer had nice clothes. There was no privacy any more, for she no longer had a small room of her own. If Granny was strict with boys she was even more strict with girls, having absorbed the Scottish Calvinist conviction that Eve was and continues to be Adam's undoing, redeemable only by a severe upbringing and unusual grace from God. So Jan entered adolescence a shapeless bundle, for the good of her own soul and that of any future husband,

and having to cope with a bunch of teasing brothers who did not understand her struggle to maintain the self-respect acquired in her first nine years of life. She was determined to become a nurse, as mother had done, and to remain at school as long as possible with that good in view.

Increasingly I was being asked what I was 'going to be', and had no answer. There was one neighbour who felt sure I would be a minister however much I denied any leaning in that direction. A friend of Uncle Tom described glowingly the cash awards and the artistic satisfaction open to a good chef. Early dreams of exploring the Amazon, or owning Wellhouse Farm, had faded away very quickly. Only two things were clear; that there was something ahead which I had been born to do, and that I must continue to study. At sixteen I had university entrance qualifications, and a Glenurquhart cousin already at Edinburgh University suggested that I should join him there. The suggestion of a Sixth Form year at the Academy with a view to sitting the University's open scholarship examination was preferable; for a whole year I could concentrate on English, Latin, French and History, dropping Mathematics and Science as I had qualified sufficiently in those subjects for university entrance. Dropping them secured seventeen free periods a week in which to work on my own at the back of a classroom.

At that point the headmaster gave me up as impossible; I never discovered what he thought of the three members of his staff who supported my proposal to divide the seventeen periods between study of Ancient Egypt, Assyria and Babylonia; the Celts; and general literature. 'D.J.', 'Pa' Duthie, and a younger teacher 'Bill' Black, supervised my work. It was the last who read and criticised notes on Akhenaton, Ashurbanipal and Gilgamesh. The Bible appeared in a new light as the events it recorded were discovered in an Egyptian or Assyrian context, which led my curiosity farther afield to the kingdoms of Elam and Persia. And who had come first, Noah or Uta-napishtim, whose stories had so much in common? Did the Law of Moses owe something to the laws of Hammurabi of Babylon? If so, what became of the story in *Exodus* of Moses on Mount Sinai receiving the two stone tablets of the Law directly from God? Even getting a second copy to make up for the first, which he had broken in a rage! The little kingdoms of Israel and Judah dwindled beside the splendour which shone in the valleys of Nile and Euphrates, where inspiration was derived from other gods than Jehovah. Who, then, was he?

When we were living in Caithness the discovery of Tutankhamun's tomb had thrilled our immediate world, and *The Children's Newspaper* had given it considerable space. One of the advantages in studying Egypt and Babylon was the amount of archaeological material available to illustrate texts, little and dull though it was then compared to the range of magnificent colour photographs available today. There was no such wealth to accompany investigation of the Celts, but Dr Douglas Hyde's *History of Irish Literature*, and a book by Lady Gregory, opened a way to the world of Cuchulain and Finn, Ossian and Deirdre, a world of which Caesar and Tacitus plainly had known next to nothing, but which Homer might have recognised as close to his own. Cuchulain and Fergus joined the heroes of Troy in my imagination; but Helen could not stand comparison with Deirdre of the Sorrows. Growing awareness of the older Celtic world and the rich body of early Irish literature was matched by increasing knowledge of Scandinavia and its Sagas. Grettir the Strong, Burnt Njal, Magnus of Orkney, Odir, Baldur, Thor and Loki; old Sea-Kings sailing to death in their blazing longships; the last thunderous battle in the Twilight of the Gods—these things for a time eclipsed all else in my imagination and gave rise to a sense of overmastering fate under which men and gods were equally constrained. Shakespeare had not gone deep enough with his lines:

As flies to wanton boys are we to the gods,
They kill us for their sport.

The gods themselves were playthings.

'And I am bound with the fierce wolf Fenrir's chain, which will never break till the end of Time has come;' I wrote in one night of self-sorrowful gloom. The mood born of adolescence and ancient hero-cycles was expressed by W. E. Henley's verses:

Out of the night that covers me,
Dark as the black pit from pole to pole,
I thank whatever gods may be
For my unconquerable soul.

Romantic gloom might come and go but did not dominate

existence. Against it was the sheer joy in an expanding world of ideas, reading, and the excitement of debate; the exhilaration of growing physical strength, the feel of one's muscles on a hillside or driving a spade, pulling a saw, hammering home a post or splitting logs. There were harvest days, working alongside my father with old Neil's household from seven or eight in the morning until dewfall maybe twelve hours later, bending, lifting, tying and stooking until eleven acres of thin oats stood in ranks waiting their time for the stackyard. As the aches of the first day grew less with practice there was pride in the accomplished work, and a closer companionship between myself and my father. As we settled down together in bed each night there was a deep feeling of sheer contentment in the few brief moments before falling asleep.

Much of the ongoing farm work was equally satisfying, not least learning to harness and control horses. At first I was nervous with them, remembering two occasions when horses had bolted, terrifying to a small child; remembering also stories of people bitten by 'difficult' horses. Nerve had to be steadied each time for the working of harnessing, until a particular horse became gradually a familiar friend. Then there was the challenge of driving loaded haycarts over a narrow bridge across a deep ditch, into which a horse and load were said to have toppled once upon a time. The first crossing of that bridge was a sweating experience followed by feelings of joy and triumph; in my own mind I had passed a test more important than the scholarship examination which lay ahead, and was accepted as a useful worker among farming people.

PART TWO

12

The day came for the journey to Edinburgh, my first trip south of the Great Glen, to sit the University's open scholarship exam. A steam train panting over Siochd and Drumochter. Snow on Cairngorm and Macdhui, a reminder of Ben Wyvis and of home. Dunkeld and Birnam—'Birnam Wood shall come to Dunsinane'—but where was Dunsinane? Lochleven's castle, unbelievingly small to have housed Mary, Queen of Scots, even although she was there only as a prisoner. Nervous excitement on crossing the River Forth, so high above water on the bridge which had featured in primary school as one of the 'Seven Wonders of the World'. At last blue and red roofs in a spring afternoon sun under Corstorphine Hill—Grandaunt Jean, small and ugly, smiling on the platform at Haymarket Station. There was lodging nearby in Roseburn among welcoming Caithness folk who had known my mother. A strong smell of gas in the flat, but nobody seemed worried. After supper there was a walk along the south side of Princes Street; suddenly, waves of scent from thousands of hyacinths unseen in the dark gardens astonished my nerves, flooding away the flat's gas-tainted air. Cocoa before bed, and my widowed hostess's two sons, older than me, wrestling strenuously on the living room floor while their mother looked on undismayed by the danger to her furniture. That could never have happened in our house! A strange place Edinburgh, with its smells of gas and flowers, was the thought as I fell asleep, sharing the younger son's bed in the living room alcove.

Next morning strengthened a feeling of unreality. From a tramcar which clanged along from Roseburn by Princes Street and North Bridge to a stop near Old College, I looked at the banks of hyacinths on one side, shops and crowded pavements on the other. There seemed to be hundreds of candidates thronging the Old College quadrangle; an incredible mob of great hairy-legged louts in shorts and school blazers from George Watson's College and other Edinburgh schools. More than two years earlier, in Inverness, my contemporaries and I had put aside shorts for long flannel trousers or plus-fours and matching jackets, worn with pride. It was extraordinary to see so many strapping figures dressed up like wee boys. Even the minority of girls in the crowd seemed junior misses compared with Highland girls. Outwardly at least the competitors were reassuringly unimpressive and the butterflies in my stomach fluttered less.

The examination papers held a major surprise of the kind more often met in day-dreams than in reality. The first question in the history papers invited an account of Britain's inhabitants before the Roman invasions. To describe Celtic Britain, drawing upon texts of Caesar and Tacitus and the work of archaeologists, was no trouble after all those periods of free study which the headmaster had derided as a foolish waste of time. What the other history questions were I have forgotten, and the enjoyable English literature questions which equally rapidly swallowed time. Not surprisingly perhaps, I was high at the weekend, when I went to visit my Glasgow cousins in their house in Pollokshields, and some more distant cousins from Caithness who lived in a flat in Bath Street. Memory retains a picture of dark furniture; of a long walk with my uncle through magnificent Victorian streets and squares on Sunday afternoon; and a story from Bath Street of someone dropping a fender from a window on the heads of Orange and Green ruffians fighting on her doorstep. On Sunday evening back to Edinburgh and boiled eggs for supper, which my over-wrought stomach promptly rejected.

In due course the results came. I was forty-third or thereabout among the successful candidates, several places higher than Alastair who had been always ahead of me in class. The Rector was somewhat at a loss for words with which to express his congratulations, and more so when, after an interview in Edinburgh, I was awarded a Cowan House residential scholarship tenable for two years with possible extension for a third.

It was an exciting summer. One Saturday Dad suggested that he and I might drive to Inverness to see a film. I was surprised and delighted by such an unusual proposal. On the way to town he remarked casually.

'What would you think about it, if I married again?'

'I think that would be a good idea', was my immediate answer. There was silence for a while, then—

'We've been invited to tea after the picture.'

'Where?'

'At Jean Dearg's place.'

'Oh!' I exclaimed, 'is she the person you're going to marry? If so, that's great!' He and Jean had been in the same class throughout school and we knew her well as a member of the Free Presbyterian congregation and an old friend of my father's family. She was strongly built, and had thick black hair and a dark tanned complexion, an attractive voice, and an air of solid quiet competence. She was a close and intelligent listener possessed usually of great patience and good humour, but able to cut short firmly anything that appeared to her either unethical or ridiculous. We liked her already and soon grew to love her, although she and my youngest brother tried each other sorely for a time. With such a stepmother at home, and scholarships won, I could set off for university with a light heart, easing by my going the pressure on space at home.

Edinburgh University at that time was small compared to what it is now. The student population was about four and a half thousand, concentrated mainly in and around the Old College, in Chambers Street, and High School Yards. A few science departments were out in isolation at West Mains Road. The colleges of agriculture, veterinary science and dentistry were separate institutions. Most students who did not live at home were in lodgings, streaming out each morning from Warrender and Marchmont and up the Middle Meadow Walk to classes, at which a certain level of attendance was obligatory. George Square was mainly residential, privately owned property, but contained a few small student halls, of which Cowan House was the largest with slightly under 120 students and teaching staff in residence. Next to it was Masson Hall, for women, with half that count of residents. (The University Library stands now on the site they occupied.) Some members of university staff owned houses in the square, notably the professors of Greek and Mathematics, Calder and Whittaker. Among other residents then or later were Sir Francis Grant, Lord Lyon King of Arms, Lady Peck, novelist sister of Father Ronald Knox; and a Lady Macleod who disapproved strongly of students lying on the grass in the Square gardens stripped to the *waist* in hot weather. Students submitted to her rebukes more tamely than a little boy whom

I remember kicking her ankles and shouting, 'My mummy says you're a nasty old woman!' Nevertheless her views on the baring of torsos to the sun would have received support from my grandmother and grandaunts and their friends, who tolerated at most arms bared to the elbow and shirts slightly open at the neck. There was no doubt in the average citizen's mind that students needed watching, having a tendency to relax moral standards; which was why there was severe restriction on visitors of the opposite sex in the two adjacent hostels. When I first knew Cowan House and Masson Hall visitors of the opposite sex were allowed brief visits in austere waiting rooms near the front doors, except twice yearly in Cowan House—for the annual dramatic performance and the Annual Dance—and once a year, I seem to remember, in Masson. Although a high wall separated the tennis courts which lay behind each house the players were open to view and to comment from overlooking windows, and from the flat roof of a two-storey T-shaped extension which ran behind the main Cowan building.

It must not be thought that Cowan was misogynist or Masson misanthropic. The idea was that each sex should keep its proper place. In Cowan, for example, the Warden had his secretary who came and went quietly each day. The Lady Housekeeper presided over a Matron, a Cook, and a crew of buxom wenches who made our beds, cleaned our rooms, and waited on us at dinner in the evening. They could be coaxed into leaving us to sleep undisturbed on those mornings when the Lady Housekeeper and Matron were not on an inspection tour. The Lady Housekeeper had her own flat on the premises, with its own front door, and there she met the House Committee from time to time and listened tolerantly to complaints or suggestions. Each evening during dinner she stood by the serving hatch in the dining room, superintending the event in corsetted dignity. Domestic staff also included two day porters and two night porters; one porter was in charge of the drink trolley from which we could purchase beer or cider at meals. Breakfast and lunch were informal, but students stood up as warden and staff residents walked in for dinner and took up their positions at the high table, sitting down only when the warden had said grace. It was, all in all, a slightly strained attempt at gracious living in the Oxbridge style; in a place founded as a reward for the work of student strike-breakers at Leith Docks in 1926.

Living in Cowan House was very comfortable. Food was abundant; three large meals daily, with never less than two courses available at each, and a snack of jam sandwiches and cocoa at 9.30 in the evening for all who might feel peckish but not hungry enough to go out for chips. There was never any lack of hot water, and the communal showers on each floor were social gathering places where people stood and soaped and chatted, especially round about eleven o'clock at night. There were no laundry rooms as each student had a laundry box in which garments went weekly to a big commercial laundry, at a modest extra cost. There was a large lounge with heavy settees and easy chairs, ideal for relaxation or for horse-play, and a smaller lounge governed by a silence rule, for reading.

Off the big lounge, in what had once been the painter Noel Paton's studio, there was a small library maintained by the residents for recreational reading. It offered to people like myself an introduction to recent literature and also made available a few books which were under legal ban at the time in this country, notably Joyce's *Ulysses* and Lawrence's *Lady Chatterley's Lover*. The first, with its unfamiliar Irish Catholic background, bored me. The second I raced through, one enjoyably erotic Sunday evening in which sensual delight was undisturbed by literary criticism. After *Lady Chatterley* the other novel by Lawrence in the library, *Sons and Lovers*, was disappointing and dull; so, for that matter were, suddenly, most novels of a serious nature. The Edinburgh life was more absorbing than fiction.

Nobody challenged this new indifference to novels, but ignorance of modern poets was another matter. A penalty of success in the scholarship competition was marked attention from some older students from Inverness and their friends, curious to investigate the new arrival on the academic scene. Three of them had me cornered one night.

'What have you been reading lately?' asked one.

'James Macpherson's *Ossian*', I answered.

'That ghastly rubbish!'

'I don't think it's rubbish!'

Battle was joined, with scornful abuse of Macpherson and myself shot from three sides and increasingly seeming, to me, to be an attack on all Gaels. The situation was made more difficult because some things said appeared, even then, not unreasonable—

but what self-respecting seventeen-year old Gael would retreat immediately from an untenable position when attacked by three nineteen or twenty-year old Lowland dogmatists? The fight broke off late at night, to be resumed next day.

I had not read Yeats's later poetry! Knew nothing of T. S. Eliot! Had never heard of Ezra Pound, or Auden or Spender! My education was indeed faulty. Would I listen to this?

> Let us go then, you and I,
> When the evening is spread out against the sky
> Like a patient etherised upon a table;
> Let us go, through certain half-deserted streets,
> The muttering retreats
> Of restless nights in one-night cheap hotels
> And sawdust restaurants with oyster-shells:
> Streets that follow like a tedious argument
> Of insidious intent
> To lead you to an overwhelming question . . .
> Oh, do not ask 'What is it?'
> Let us go and make our visit.

The Love Song of J. Alfred Prufrock

'That's no love song!' I snorted. The reader took no notice:

> In the room the women come and go
> Talking of Michelangelo.
>
> The yellow fog that rubs its back upon the window-panes,
> The yellow smoke that rubs its muzzle on the window-
>   panes,
> Licked its tongue into the corners of the evening,
> Lingered upon the pools that stand in drains,
> Let fall upon its back the soot that falls from chimneys,
> Slipped by the terrace, made a sudden leap,
> And seeing that it was a soft October night,
> Curled once about the house, and fell asleep.

The voice continued, insistently disregarding my romantic scorn. When the three evangelists at last retired I went down to the library and removed the volume of Eliot to my room to look over it quietly alone. The man had something, I began to admit grudgingly to myself. I liked:

I have heard the mermaids singing, each to each.

I do not think that they will sing to me.

I have seen them riding seaward on the waves
Combing the white hair of the waves blown back
When the wind blows the water white and black.

We have lingered in the chambers of the sea
By sea-girls wreathed with seaweed red and brown
Till human voices wake us and we drown.

Sweeney Among the Nightingales was inexplicably fascinating and the last six lines were soon in my memory:

The nightingales are singing near
The Convent of the Sacred Heart,

And sang within the bloody wood
When Agamemnon cried aloud
And let their liquid siftings fall
To stain the stiff dishonoured shroud.

Agamemnon's tragedy in a new setting indeed!

Later, one of the three pundits made me aware of a writer known as Hugh MacDiarmid, whose real name it appeared was Christopher Murray Grieve although he wished to sound more Celtic than he actually was. His lyrics, in two small books, *Sangschaw* and *Penny Wheep*, straightway had far more appeal than Eliot's *Love Song of J. Alfred Prufrock* or the soon-to-become tedious declamation of 'Ossian' Macpherson. I began to listen to the older students and to learn from them, and through them came to meet eventually writers and thinkers of the modern Scottish Renaissance. Everything had to be re-examined, for all that had been familiar in literature, politics, and religion, was under fire from some quarter. Argument could spring up during a meal, during morning coffee or afternoon tea in one of the restaurants close to the Old College, but especially during the 9.30 supper in Cowan House, whence it might continue, sustained by coffee and tobacco, far into the night in someone's room, occasionally even to breakfast time. This was life and classrooms were dull, the one exception for me, as for many, being that in which Professor H. J. C. Grierson meditated aloud upon English and other literature, with copious quotation—his notes pushed away after the first few minutes.

Like other Scottish students with Higher English behind them, I had a factual knowledge of English literature from *Beowulf* to the twentieth century, and was familiar with the outlines of British history from 55 BC to 1919. Grierson and his staff encouraged a more critical reading of familiar texts. They drew attention also to Scottish literature, and Harvey Wood provided a short introduction to Scottish writers from the fourteenth century to the twentieth. Grierson was styled 'Professor of Rhetoric and English Literature' and considered it part of his responsibility to deliver ten or so lectures each year on language and style. There was little drudgery associated with what was known as First Ordinary English, and interest kindled in the lecture-room was stimulated further by the company of younger members of staff in coffee shops or tearooms, and at the weekly meetings of the English Literature Society, one of the bigger and more active among the dozens of student societies which were a major feature in the academic landscape.

In the first year I read only one other subject, British History; inescapable morning drudgery; attendance cards were collected; worse, I was in the professor's tutorial and my face familiar to his inspecting eye. The professor stood, short and tubby, with a long pointer in his hand, in a pepper-and-salt suiting, like a parody of the figure of Britannia on the coinage, and plodded through a heavy paraphrase of the prescribed textbook, T. F. Tout's *Advanced History of Great Britain* Vol. III. Basil Williams's own field of study was the expansion of the British Empire. He had experienced some active involvement with its expansion in South Africa and had come to prepare us for various forms of imperial service at home or abroad, to teach us what we ought to know as good British citizens rather than to train us as professional students of history. I thought it would be best to concentrate on literature and to abandon all thought of a degree in history. Then came the shattering news that Grierson was to be succeeded by John Dover Wilson. Pleasant man though the latter proved to be, I had no wish to study under him, having heard him once lecturing romantically on Rupert Brooke and knowing his preoccupation with printers' errors in Shakespearean quartos.

The lesser evil, it seemed for a little while, was to remain in the field of diplomacy, wars, and constitutions.

Academically that first year at university was disastrous. I sailed through, mainly on what I had acquired at school, and finished with First Class Merit Certificates in English Literature, Scottish Literature and British History, together with a variety of absorbing interests mostly unfavourable to anything in the way of formal study. From then on I would do just enough work to retain scholarships, and seldom more. I was free from the responsibility of the previous four years at home and able to enjoy myself in ways impossible at home; puppy off the leash, stirk on Spring grass, living each day with no time to bother about tomorrows, fed intellectually by older students who appreciated such professors as A. E. Taylor in Moral Philosophy, Kemp Smith in Logic and Metaphysics, Edmund Whittaker in Mathematics, and Donald Francis Tovey in Music. Every second Sunday during term Tovey conducted the Reid Orchestra in the Usher Hall, students admitted for sixpence. The Scottish Orchestra was there at other times, also with concessionary rates for students; me, musical illiterate, walking away in a trance after first hearing Beethoven's 'Pastoral' Symphony, the 'Emperor' Concerto, Schubert's 'Unfinished' Symphony, or Holst's Hymn of Jesus in St Mary's Cathedral, to name a few that remain unforgettable in memory. Live performances reduced the gramophone to inferior status, a valuable aid to memory but, especially in those pre-stereophonic days, no adequate substitute for live performances in the Usher Hall. Nevertheless records played over and over again helped towards clearer perception of form. 'When will you get tired of playing Brahms' Fourth?' asked a musician friend and neighbour wearily one day.

The Free Presbyterian minister at home had recommended the study of Logic, which accounted for my registration in the second year as a member of Kemp Smith's First Ordinary class. Logic meant traditional formal logic:

All men are mortal.
Socrates is a man.
Therefore Socrates is mortal.

(Water, water wallflower! . . . We must all die! . . . Man goeth to his long home, and the mourners go about the streets. And my mind and imagination wandered easily.) There was an essay to write on the pre-Socratic thinkers; no problem. I wept privately reading Plato's account of the death of Socrates, but put his *Republic* aside for another day. The second essay to be attempted was on knowledge, or man and nature perhaps— what, precisely, is long forgotten. After two days in an easy chair, feet up on another, something of sufficient length was written. 'This is a strange essay,' said my tutor, brow wrinkled. 'I find it difficult to know how to mark it. It is full of profound conclusions with nothing to show how you have arrived at them. You have obviously been reading widely.' I disclaimed such industry truthfully, denied any direct knowledge of the writers whose influence he claimed to discern, but saw with some annoyance that he was unconvinced. Awarding marks and certificates was important in the system, and he had to be fair. After a mental struggle he wrote on the paper 'B + −' and after that I drifted out of philosophy without discovering what the 'important conclusions' were. Harry Rothwell, lecturing in European History, was more encouraging to attempts to think, but understandably wanted to see thinking grow from acquaintance with facts. His lecturing style would never have attracted crowds but he was a scholar concerned for historical truth, whatever that might be, and for the welfare of his students. It was thanks to him that the second year was not totally an academic waste.

George Davie had been told at Dundee High School: 'You are here to learn what you ought to know. You can begin to think for yourself when you go to University.' But the latter seemed not greatly interested in promotion of original thought among adolescents. A rare few among us might be awarded First Class Honours, after four dutiful years in the Faculty of Arts or the Faculty of Science; a minority might then tackle the rarefied summits of Oxbridge, where true grammarians were trained, and the choicest candidates for the higher ranks of government service. Glenurquhart had produced an Oxford professor of Celtic, John Fraser, although he had produced but little after settling there. Other glens could boast of knights or barons laureated after service in some distant colony or dominion. All had their share of clergymen, doctors and teachers. Many students in their first year knew already to what service or

My mother with me at Beauly, 1917

My younger brother David with Jan (centre) and myself (right)

My mother

Granny Ross

Grandfather Ross

Mary Clyne

My father and mother

My father in France

My father: Wick, 1913

My class at Inverness Academy (Second from right back row)

My sister Jan

My brother David

Myself as a student at Blackfriars, Oxford, in 1945

Myself taken whilst Rector of Edinburgh University, 1979–82

Myself (right) with brothers Tom (centre) and David, 1984

distinction they aspired, and worked with appropriate application, although sometimes over an astonishing number of years before their final graduation. Universities were patient and tolerant communities, allowing for slow maturation of doctors or lawyers especially, as long as they could pay their way as students. Twelve or even thirteen years might pass before a doctor was let loose among the public, and a very good doctor he might prove to be in the end, despite the time he had occupied in the affairs of the University Union, or the Students' Representative Council, or on the sports field, or simply at the Union bar.

In the case of some among us the certainties were negative. We had no desire for colonial service, no wish to be doctors, lawyers, ministers or teachers. We were restless adolescents who had moved at sixteen or seventeen years of age from a sheltered, highly disciplined environment into an unfamiliar state of freedom and, except for the families and schools from which we had come, few people were much concerned about how we used that freedom or where we finished. Or so it seemed for a time.

13

First-year students were expected to be back in Cowan House by 11.30 pm unless given permission from Warden or Sub-Warden to be out later. Some of the older students appeared to feel that more was needed to keep new students in their place. The first manifestation of big brotherliness was the 'Freshers' Concert' held near the beginning of the academic year. Performance at it was compulsory, on pain of debagging and a cold bath. An unsatisfactory performance was met by showers of dried peas or shouts of 'Take your trousers down!' I decided that my performance would be short; it must contain an element of surprise initially and then subtly draw the audience into participation. So I sprang on to the table with alacrity and launched into the Gaelic song 'Aig posadh piuthar lain Bhan': surprise, attention; miraculously I remained in key, and went hilariously into the chorus, 'I hu-ro-ho! I ho-ro-ho!' Laughter from the audience which launched into its own lively variation: 'A whore! oh! ho! A whore! oh! ho!' After the second verse it was clearly safe to jump down and join the spectactors.

There was a small amount of bullying, in one instance rising from snobbish dislike of what would later be known as a 'mature student', from a large working-class family, who was financing his career in the university by free-lance journalism. His adult disdain of 'childish behaviour', and his casual, passive attitude towards cold baths or debagging, soon defused the zeal of his persecutors. More troublesome to younger first year students were some hefty characters, chiefly from the medical faculty, who liked to round off their weekly boozing session by raiding some inoffensive character who was asleep when they came back to the house. Initially it was to deal with them that the 'Holy League of the Sacred Shofar' came into existence, a secret band of what were outwardly quiet or even timid-looking students. Its aim was to teach the disturbers a lesson, but in such a way that there could be no identification of the agents involved and small danger of retaliation.

Two of the most regular disturbers were selected for the League's best attention. They were known to be looking forward to a dance one night and duly left the house dressed immaculately and formally for the occasion. A carefully detailed programme of action had been drawn up by the nine members of the League; each had a specific part to play, with emphasis on strict timing, to a split second almost. That evening no one else in the house heard or saw anything unusual. The two leaders of the Holy League were in full view for most of the evening, usually reading in the lounge, at one point the centre of horseplay. When the two disturbers returned from the dance, a few hours after midnight, the room which they shared was totally bare, stripped even of light fittings. It contained only a notice on the floor which said something like 'Leave others in peace and you will be left in peace.' The search for the room's contents was concluded hours later when daylight made it possible. Sections of the beds, bookshelves, chairs, books and pictures were hidden all over the house; clothes were hung on a line across the garden; but nobody outside the nine had seen or heard anything happen. The operation proved highly effective; the disturbers stopped disturbing. There was, however, a new problem. 'The Holy League of the Sacred Shofar' had enjoyed itself and wanted more fun.

It became responsible for a series of practical jokes and was seen as a challenge by amateur detectives, one or two of whom were bent on proving that I was the director of mischief, however covered by alibis, whose regular production was of course in itself highly suspicious to students of crime fiction. 'Don't try any of your tricks on me!' said a disapproving member of staff (later to be Professor of Mathematics in another university), growling before a cloud of witnesses one evening during supper. The challenge was irresistible. Some weeks later two of us stood engaging him in conversation during another supper-time. At the appointed moment a student car drew up in the lane at the rear of the building. A bundle was handed up quickly to the flat roof of the T-extension, rushed across the roof and attached to a rope let down from a window two storeys higher up in the main block. Seconds later a placard appeared on the notice-board outside the big lounge:

EDINBURGH UNIVERSITY SCANDAL!
BASHED BEAUTY IN LECTURER'S BED.
A CUNNING RUSE?

A student of unquestioned innocence wandered into the lounge and remarked 'I think somebody's attempting a rather obscure joke about you, Dr Ruse!' And then, to the Sub-warden in a guileless voice: 'Have you seen the notice-board, sir?' The Sub-warden went to look at it, others followed. Another simple student started what became a rush to view the bed, Dr Ruse, accompanied by the Sub-warden, bringing up the rear with dignity, a cup of cocoa still in his hand. Pushing through the laughing crowd in his room he sat down with a gasp on the edge of the bed, then turned and said, 'You little devil!' as a camera flashed into action. The photograph proved beautifully clear when printed. Tucked up in the supposed misogynist's bed was 'the Lady Sylvia Bathwick,' a life-size female dummy which had been donated to a float in Rag Week by a fashion shop in Princes Street and had been lying for weeks in an Old College basement. There were threats of revenge, but the victim on reflection took the sporting view expected of a popular member of the house. After all, as he ruefully admitted, he had brought the Lady Sylvia on himself!

The League could have become a public nuisance but after two terms it faded away quietly. Its minutes were burnt during the war and will not embarrass the now eminent English divine who suggested its name—he was studying Hebrew at the time—or the equally eminent civil servant who played an effective part in some of its action, his poker face and sober habits keeping him beyond any suspicion. Practical jokes were a phenomenon of the period, staple matter in juvenile fiction and almost expected of adolescents. Most people soon grew out of them at university, and the members of the League were fortunately no exception.

As with practical jokes so with horseplay, of which there was a fair amount in British universities at that time. In Edinburgh the annual Charities' Week especially was marked by high spirits, sometimes viewed sourly by citizens. Cowan House students had a store of several dozen pink and white checked cotton frocks, distributed without concern for how they fitted and, on most people, anticipating the mini-skirt by some decades. Bus-loads of transvestites poured into the Border towns rattling collection boxes, heavily and crudely painted faces offering protection against instant recognition, but drawing occasionally ribald cries from Border youth. Two weeks of raids drained away my enthusiasm for such ploys but left behind a certain affection for the folk of Hawick, Galashiels and Selkirk and a fair knowledge of their geography which would be useful later. Charities' Week activities were marked generally by good behaviour and harmless jokes; although Sir Will Y. Darling threatened my edition of *Euragonnah*, the Week's magazine, with an interdict, being offended by a cartoon which celebrated his firm's refusal to advertise in our pages; and there was a misguided and clumsy private effort one year to kidnap and hold to ransom the actress Miss Renée Houston, who was much alarmed and not in the least amused.

14

On the whole, however, student life flowed uneventfully. As lectures lost significance the days were marked out by mealtimes and by morning coffee and afternoon tea. In the evenings there might be pub gatherings, or chip suppers in 'Bonzo's' in Nicolson Square, or 'De Marco's' in Forrest Road, after the weekly meeting of some society. Pub gatherings were all-male, as respectable women did not enter the tobacco-clouded sawdust and spittoon world of the average Scottish pub at that time. Male chauvinism governed drinking in the university itself. There was a Women's Union purveying tea and coffee; and there was a Men's Union, known simple as the University Union, in whose bar rugby songs and bothy ballads mingled, Kirriemuir and Oscar Wilde being best-known names. Occasionally some of us organised a special mixed evening in the Peacock Inn in Newhaven where great platters of excellent fish were eaten with bread and butter and washed down with wine. Those were hilarious evenings where we seemed, to ourselves, to sparkle with wit and knowledge in the tradition of the Scottish Enlightenment, or the *Noctes Ambrosianae* of Christopher North and the Ettrick Shepherd. Freud, whose *Psychopathology of Everyday Life* circulated among us then as the latest discovery, helped the development of a personally directed in-group bawdry. Still ruled by a code which said premarital sex was wrong, and which even discouraged kissing before an engagement was announced, we noted polymorphous perversion among our fellow adolescents and referred to a homosexual member of our group as 'Pansy', behind his back of course since his tongue was sharp and he would retaliate with Freud more skilfully than most. We watched knowingly as a callow public-school boy was guided by his seniors towards heterosexuality; but we had little to say about the small minority who were rumoured to enjoy illicit sex now and again at weekends. Two of our younger friends, afraid of being identified if they went to prostitutes in Edinburgh, hired a car and drove to London in search of experience. They left on Friday and returned crestfallen on Sunday, having been told by two ladies whom they accosted on the Embankment not to be silly boys and to go back home.

Despite Freud, politics played a larger part than sex in our conversation. Student politics early caught my attention, as I listened in the first term to older students in Cowan House fulminating against a clique of Old Watsonians and members of the Student Christian Movement which, they said, controlled the Students' Representative Council with a firm conservative grip. 'Why not throw them out?' I said and organised a campaign to that end. The first step was to identify potential 'progressives', and to secure seats quietly for as many of them as possible, as student society representatives, before the election of year and faculty representatives was due to take place. In this way we captured some thirteen or so seats before publishing a leaflet which denounced the existing state of affairs and invited votes for 'progressive' candidates, whose names and con- stituencies were listed. Speeches were made from the balustrades of Old College and other vantage points. More leaflets were published. The Progressives were accused of cheapening SRC business by bringing party divisions and tactics into the election. On the morning of polling day I was kidnapped and locked in a shed somewhere near South Queensferry, until polling stations closed. The kidnappers were George Pottinger, Morris Carstairs, Andrew Maclaren Young and W. A. C. Matheson, who provided a splendid tea when they released me that evening. Their action was a major political blunder. Suddenly the 'progressive' campaign made sense to some who had doubted its argument. *The Evening News* had headlines. Wavering supporters shot indignantly into action. Our group swept to victory, and soon established another clique. It fell apart a few months later after a row over an article in *The Student* which was censured as obscene by the SRC; the editor resigned, mistakenly in my view; a middle, more pragmatic group assumed control of student affairs. After two years on the SRC I decided not to seek re-election although there was a campaign still to be fought, against the Principal's plan to house more and more students in halls of residence. To some of us these plans if achieved would result in reduced contact between students and citizens, and undesirably tighter control over student life by university administration. We were opposed totally to the creation of a 'University City', and defeated the candidate for the Rectorship of the University, Dr Donald Pollock, whose financial support was relied upon to make the Principal's dream come true. The election of Emeritus Professor Sir Herbert Grierson as Rector delayed only for a few years the election of Dr Pollock and the establishment of the Pollock Halls.

Interest in student domestic politics faded in the light of national and international affairs between 1934 and 1939. In the University Union political debates drew large numbers of students, grouped in major party allegiance—Conservative, Socialist, Liberal, in that order of strength in my first year. All good Socialists became readers of Left Book Club volumes; meaty stuff compared to the Right Book Club's weak response, it seemed to us. Not that Socialists spent much time on Right Book Club publications. The Holy Office and the Inquisition could not have been more impatient with us who listened to theological deviants than were students who aspired to political leadership with those who listened seriously to their opponents. A friend who returned at the beginning of the Spanish Civil War, after a year in Spain, soon refused to talk about that country at all, having been insulted from Right and Left when he reported truthfully what he personally had seen or heard. It was not only Leninists who subordinated fact to dogma. The political world held many crusaders, with white, black, brown, green, red or blue shirts, for whom some body of dogma was beyond all question. They were, as the old people would have said, like the geese in harvest-time, hearing nothing which did not accord with their own preoccupation.

My father's politics were in the Scottish Labour tradition of Keir Hardie, but coloured by disillusionment resulting from experience of corruption in local affairs. If socialist representatives proved corrupt, acting not for sake of the common weal but from personal greed and selfishness, what hope could there be of ever securing a just society? Behind the political struggle lay, for every human being, a personal struggle which must be faced, a struggle towards integrity and an intelligent recognition of one's place in the commonwealth of Man. He looked to education as the only and indispensable means of achieving this ideal. Reason, science; the new social sciences, especially psychology; the parliament of man, the federation of the world; these terms were bright coin in his early manhood, and in my childhood. He spoke about them less as the dictators rose higher, but they were still eloquent for me in my first years as a student; and I believed that there was a natural goodness in men, which could be reached, if only they were freed from hunger and the fear of war. Socialism and pacifism, practised together, could not fail—if only one country would take courage and show the way.

Like many other students, therefore, I worked to secure signatures for the Peace Pledge, the solemn renunciation of war which was signed by millions of British citizens. Some of the city's worst slums were given to students to canvass, and part of the tenements in St James's Square fell to me. Its solid looking masonry was familiar from outside, and there were distressingly familiar sights on its pavements. In Edinburgh's inner city at that time drunk bodies collapsed in the streets were a common sight. There were also people grotesquely deformed; dwarfs with bow legs, or with great heads on small bodies; shapeless women whose bodies were a travesty of the human form; children with old grey faces, and the evidence of malnutrition blatant in their twisted limbs; and, sometimes, conditions which I learned only much later were attributable to congenital syphilis.

I had not seen inside slum tenements. There were small children from them to play with once a week, at the University Settlement, who smelt sometimes as the tinker children had done in Caithness; but there had been nothing in Caithness like the dark warrens inside St James's Square, with their broken floorboards and gaping stair windows, the inadequate supply of communal lavatories long past cleaning and, worst of all, an atmosphere of fear. My own fear would swell when a knock on a door was the signal for scuffling behind it, followed by utter silence; or when a door was opened a few inches, to be slammed at once; or when steps came along behind in the semi-darkness, or a face peered close to mine with, or without, a sharp question or an abusive remark. I was shamed briefly into comparative calm when an old woman threw her door wide open, to show a cared-for room that shone as brightly as her own face. That was a unique experience which, at the time, only emphasised the inhuman conditions in which so many human beings lived. Peace or war—would it make any great difference to them? Were those perhaps right who said reform was impossible, and that nothing but violent revolution could bring deep or lasting change? Who would make a better society when the present one was overthrown of which we were all part? All in varying degrees corrupted no doubt.

The children. A girl child, four years old, with the 'come-hither' technique of the street women in the poorer beats of the city. A little boy with a taste for drawing smaller boys into the tea-pantry in the Settlement building and then beating them up. Was it an accident that one day he was seen shutting the door behind him with a gleeful look, having turned on the gas, and leaving a two-year-old in the room? Innocence was destroyed at an early age for some. These two victims of society could not play, but the majority of the two to five-year-old boys and girls who were left in my care for one and a half hours on Wednesday afternoons played with the same spirit as my youngest cousins, and liked equally piggy-back rides and tag games. But for many there was a background of heavy violence, as well as hunger and dirt.

15

Violence in various forms could not be ignored in that decade of totalitarian brutality, gang warfare in some places, terrorism in others. A good friend from Inverness was killed when a suitcase left by Irish terrorists exploded in Victoria Station in London; ironic tragedy for him and his friends, since he was in sympathy with Irish aspirations. Gandhi seemed to point a way of non-violence, but I wondered how he and his friends would fare under Stalin or Hitler, or under any régime unfettered by Christian scruples or liberal humanism. How easily principles vanished under pressure of events was shown in my own behaviour. One night, as I lay in bed reading, a prolonged series of bumps shook the ceiling of my room in Cowan House until, with some annoyance, I put on a dressing-gown and went to investigate. Three or four Scottish students were watching with apparent amusement as a beefy German exchange student, dressed only in shorts, jumped repeatedly on a slightly built, drunk Scot, knocking him to the floor again and again, each time he tried to get up. The German was a fanatical Nazi, a picture specimen of Nordic youth, blond and muscular, a successful product of Hitler's youth movement. I disliked him personally, and on seeing what was happening shouted a challenge which brought him after me as I shot along corridors and downstairs to a dark passage in the basement where I turned, grappled, and brought him down with a side headlock and a hip throw, followed by an arm-lever against the joint which made him scream and scream again. His violent efforts to break free only increased the agony, until he submitted abjectly and begged for mercy. So much for my pacifism, and for recognition of Christ in every man. The truth was that I hated him, and would at that moment have broken his arm readily, had I not feared the consequences in law.

Now and again the deeper roots of anger and aggression were laid bare disconcertingly. One evening two of us were wrestling furiously. At last I had the other student at my mercy and, looking down at his face, realised suddenly that he had become a substitute for my father. As he lay helpless he saw the shock in my face, and was puzzled to know what had caused it, and why I refused to wrestle any more that evening. There seemed also to be some connection between aggression and sexual frustration, although I did not try to work it out; fighting seemed to reduce sexual tension. In the course of one exceptionally strenuous encounter two of us crashed about a large double room, over armchairs and beds, and at one stage under a bed. It was then that I had my first experience of orgasm, pleasurable but hardly noticed as the fight continued, until I eventually won.

That experience was different from the fun of chasing and tickling Jeanie in the hayfield, which involved the use of strength but was not fiercely aggressive. Aggressiveness was the problem in the world; the aggressive feelings of individuals and society which menaced people's safety; my own vicious feeling towards Kemnitz and another Nazi student; the extraordinary ferocity in the speeches of a Quaker lady active in the Peace Pledge campaign; the stories of sheer brutality associated with gang warfare in America and with razor gangs nearer home; the indiscriminate murder committed by terrorist groups; the Italian invasion of Abyssinia, the Spanish Civil War; Hitler. What

answer could there be? Gandhi's non-violent tactics depended
for effectiveness on his own personal ascetic discipline, on the
discipline of unarmed Sikh supporters passively facing police
charges, and on a certain degree of moral restraint on the part of
the British authorities. There seemed to be less and less moral
restraint in the world. Why should there by any? Stags and bulls
ruled their herds by might. Why should not might be right among
human beings also? Genetic principles suggested that we breed
from the fittest stock and eliminate runts. That was sound sense
when dealing with cattle and sheep, pigs and dogs. Christians or
humanists who cried out about 'man's inhumanity to man' were
the voice of weakness, afraid of facing squarely the fact of human
animality, and of applying scientific knowledge to ensure more
rapid evolution of a race superior to any in existence. But for
what? Why try to change the situation? While there was some
pleasure in living why not continue to live, as comfortably as
one could? There were no heroic phantasies in the animal
kingdom, neither Marxist nor Christian dreams of a glorious
future, no other problem than that of survival. The debate went
round and round in the head. When I entered my third year at
the university I had given up going to church, working at the
Settlement, or taking study seriously. The village schoolmaster
remarked to one of my younger brothers that he was sorry to
hear that I had 'taken to drink'. When his sorrow was reported a
shrug of the shoulders seemed comment enough, from one who
drank more than some and less than others and could not afford
the amount of liquor necessary to get really drunk.

Disassociation from church did not mean the disappearance
of religion from life. There was a notable issue of churchgoers
from Cowan House on Sundays, and a strong Student Christian
Movement study group existed among the residents. It included
as steady members three future Presbyterian ministers, two
future Congregationalist ministers, a future Catholic priest, two
medical students and an agnostic mathematician. Others, like
myself, joined its weekly meetings now and again. In my
memory it is more vividly associated with tobacco than with
theology. Most members smoked pipes, heavily clouding the
atmosphere with the fumes of 'Four Square' tobacco as the
evening wore on. Pipes were recommended as cheaper than
cigarettes and, resolving to give up cigarettes, I bought a pipe
one day, and at that evening's meeting filled it carefully, and sat

back well content that it was drawing smoothly. Drinking beer or whisky had never created the fine feeling of maturity which that pipe produced for perhaps fifteen minutes. The first feeling of unease came suddenly and increased with appalling speed. One of the future ministers noticed what was happening, and springing to his feet seized me by the shoulder, propelling me to a lavatory just as my eyes shut out the spinning world, and my insides erupted. That first cheap pipe had not been burned in, and the effect of its varnish on an inexperienced smoker was indescribably horrible at the time; but soon to be remembered with wry amusement.

Another event was far more painful. The Student Christian Movement organised Sunday morning services in the wards of the nearby Royal Infirmary; hymns, bible readings, an address. I accepted an invitation to give an address one morning and prepared carefully something or other about suffering with Christ. Standing looking at the sick, in their freshly tidied beds, I was struck by the knowledge that I had no business to be there. The right thing would have been to withdraw at least from speaking, instead of blundering on with red-faced awareness of the impertinence of what I was doing, and the cowardliness of continuing to do it with the patient eyes of the sick all around, a captive audience for adolescent presumption. My friend David would never have done such a thing. He was a contemporary who died of peritonitis in his second year at university. When we first met I disliked him. He was trim and quiet, slightly built with pale, sharp features, looking like a businessman with his neat grey suit and gold-rimmed spectacles. One evening, after watching horse-play in the common room, he said in his precise voice, 'I see you know a little about wrestling. I think I would like to take you on.' It sounded absurd that such a slender lightweight should challenge someone at least 35 lb heavier than himself, but when he stripped for action there was visible evidence of wiry muscle. He had not mentioned membership of a well-known wrestling club, not his experience of wrestling with a heavily muscled and expert elder brother. He demonstrated clearly on our first encounter that superior weight and brute force could not defeat speed and skill combined with supple strength, and intelligence. Wrestling with him was like playing chess. His intelligence directed each move with several possible sequences in mind; mind and muscle were perfectly co-ordinated and his effort was directed with unvarying coolness and total concentration. There was no question of my beating him, for always he had me on the defensive, until his lessons were absorbed sufficiently for our rôles to be reversed, occasionally. It was he who made me into a good wrestler dependent more on mind than muscle, and gave me the skill which defeated Kemnitz.

David was deeply religious, without any ostentation. He was an outstanding classical scholar, with a quiet methodical approach to any argument, in marked contrast to my passionate rhetoric. When he invited me to stay at his home in Fife it became clear that he derived his approach to discussion from his father, a well-read headmaster and lay preacher in the Churches of Christ, and from his mother, a warm, intelligent, competent person; both good listeners. Two brothers, one older and one younger, and a younger sister, completed a lively, close-knit family, which took me to itself, especially after the shock of David's sudden death. There was a gentle attempt to guide me towards their own religious position which seemed to require no credal confession other than 'I believe in Jesus Christ,' leaving it to the individual to interpret that statement as he found best. Through the family's friendship I was introduced to a wider range of religious thought, and thanks to them spent two weeks on vacation at Selly Oak in Birmingham, as a guest of one of the theological colleges there and with access to the Cadbury Library, whose shelves contained much that was new, including the collected writings of Lenin, in English, and the works of Berdyaev. It was too much all at once. I had been reading for years. There appeared no end to reading. Selly Oak gave new force to the sighs of *Ecclesiastes*: 'Of making of many books there is no end; and much study is a weariness of the flesh.' *Ecclesiastes* and Omar Khayyam were at one: 'Vanity of vanities; all is vanity.' Let it all go. Why worry?

Books could be pushed aside, even if one lived in a university, but not events. Unemployment and poverty were evident in the streets. 'This is now *our* Elizabethan Age,' wrote my Japanese pen-friend, setting out for war in China. The League of Nations which had failed to halt Japan, failed to halt or even modify Italian aggression in Ethiopia in 1935. Next year civil war began in an already disturbed Spain and before long people one knew were involved on one side or the other. There were refugees in

Edinburgh from Spain, from Germany. People argued about whether Hitler's *Mein Kampf* should be taken seriously. In Russia the heroes of the Revolution were being exterminated as traitors. There were arguments about that, too, full of passion, but, as in all the arguments, there was the nagging question of what was going on in fact. What did we really know? And how could we judge what was good or bad? There had been photographs of Mussolini, stripped to the waist, working among harvesters on land reclaimed from the Pontine Marshes. On cinema newsreels we saw evidence that Hitler was tackling unemployment and restoring health and purpose to young Germans. People muttered that it was time our politicians took a leaf out of Hitler's book, or got their shirts off like Mussolini. Were not Hitler, Mussolini and Stalin all Socialists in spite of their differences? It was not at all easy to distinguish clearly between foreign politicians; especially since Nazis and Stalinists would lie on principle. Were our own politicians more reliable? People, whether active in politics or not, selected data to suit their emotion and the roots of emotion were deep and far from obvious. Perhaps Freud had the key to politics, not the philosophers or economists. A student in the house was going round the bend, but the warden brushed aside the anxiety expressed by three of us, without examining the reasons for it; then one day a door had to be forced and the student was removed to a mental hospital for treatment. We were angry with the warden for not listening seriously, and could not understand his attitude. It was another illustration of how people in responsible positions would not face facts under their very noses. 'Of course, it was to be expected!' remarked one of the older readers of Freud; 'as soon as he heard of masturbation in public the shutters came down. He simply did not want to know!'

Man's 'inhumanity' was inescapable. Evidence of it was everywhere; in some of our everyday behaviour towards each other, in the slums of Edinburgh, in the sickening violence inflicted on the Ethiopians by Italian technology, in Spanish atrocities. Other animals were different from us. Stoats and weasels loose in a poultry run would kill and kill until all the chickens were dead. Shrews would fight each other to the death. But only man went through long systematic programmes of torture of members of his own kind, and killed them by hundreds of thousands. No other animal killed on such a scale and so uselessly. Not even stoats could match our blood lust.

Discussion went round and round in the head; guts tightened; tension was relieved by talking, by drinking, and sometimes by wrestling to exhaustion. The girls in our circle appeared somehow more relaxed than the boys, when we met for coffee or tea, as we did most days. Elizabeth, Anna, Jean, Helen, Joan and Margaret made life seem less pointless in their company. It was not that they ignored events or failed to recognise problems. They discussed socialism and pacifism as well as anyone, but they were less aggressive, less bitter in their manner, and sounded as though they had more hope for the future. Elizabeth was two years or so older than me, but much older in wisdom, and I sat at her feet literally and metaphorically in her house or garden, and talked with a freedom there was with no one else. If anything our friendship deepened after it become obvious that we were moving towards marriage with other people. She had a faith which accepted the idea of marriage and a family with Christian optimism in spite of the times. I loved children, and was attracted to one particular girl, a marvellous singer called Kitty Macleod, but with no such optimism. My father was in sympathy with my position. He said that if he were my age he would not wish to bring children into our world, one so plainly growing worse to live in. The thought in my head was the twelfth verse of Matthew, chapter 19:

> For there are some eunuchs, which were so born from their mother's womb: and there are some eunuchs, which were made eunuchs of men: and there be eunuchs, which have made themselves eunuchs for the kingdom of heaven's sake. He that is able to receive it, let him receive it.

My father and I spoke of politics sometimes during vacations, when working together in the garden or trapping rabbits. He was opposed to war, but thought it was probably inevitable, greatly though he hated it. He had gone into the 1914–18 war like so many young men from the Highlands, with a romantic vision of military adventure and joy in the male cameraderie of a Highland regiment. He came out with a fierce loyalty to his fellow infantrymen, but with a mixture of pity or contempt for many officers—'boys whose ability to play games at school was supposed to make them suitable to direct fighting!' He had stories of tragic blunders which naturally had never received publicity. A man 'died in action' whether killed by British, French or German guns. After the war Dad had shared the dream of so many people, that a more just and peaceful order would be established, a socialist republic offering equal opportunities for all its members, with free education and medical care available to everyone; with science and invention banishing ignorance, disease and poverty. He had no hatred or dislike of Germans as a result of that first world war, but very strong feelings against imperialism and capitalism anywhere. He said little at home about his two bouts of rheumatic fever, or the mud and vermin of trench warfare; that to him would have been too much like self-pity. Once, when someone complained that mutton broth was greasy, he snorted: 'Men would have been glad of that in the trenches, where soup was often so thick with fat that only English soldiers would eat it. The Scots preferred to go hungry!' For fuller impressions of 1914–18 I depended on Erich Remarque's *All Quiet on the Western Front* and Henri Barbusse's *Under Fire*; the first on Dad's recommendation, the second discovered by myself.

In much of our time together during vacations there was, however, little talking. Speech was limited usually to essential communication, when working at something. It was similar when walking, especially on the hills, when it was immensely satisfactory and relaxing to fall in with my father's long steady stride, which covered ground so rapidly without any suggestion of hurry. When we paused on some vantage point he might make some comment about past events, or weather signs, or animals, or farming methods. At times his withering contempt for incompetent smallholders or crofters was embarrassing in its harshness. He should have been a farmer or a teacher, not a shopkeeper, and his strictures on teachers and farmers reflected envy and frustration, and regret for old dreams and lost opportunities. One day at home he was doodling apparently with pencil and paper for some time. At last he looked up and announced wryly, as he relit his pipe, how many thousands of pounds his father and himself had spent on whisky and tobacco respectively; money enough to have sent him to university or launched him into farming. But increasingly he seemed content, with my stepmother's love and understanding, and her efficient management of domestic affairs, making life sweeter. Sundays during vacation were much as before. My stepmother was a regular church attender, critical of ministers and of lay-preachers in a detached way, with her personal devotion to Christ completely unruffled by them. My father went to church more often because of her, and so I had peaceful hours alone on many Sundays.

16

Back in Edinburgh I rarely went to church. Occasionally a fellow student invited me to go to some church on a Sunday morning and I went, out of curiosity or friendship. During my first year I had gone to the Free Presbyterian Church in Gilmore Place fairly frequently, if unenthusiastically, knowing nobody at the beginning of the year, and nobody at the end. Sermon tasting here and there in city churches such as St Giles', or St John's at the West end of Princes Street, or St George's West, did nothing to lessen the attraction of quiet Sunday mornings spent in a deep armchair, beside a radiator, browsing through newspapers and adding to the tobacco smoke which pleasantly misted the big lounge of Cowan House. After the usual enormous Sunday lunch there might be a comatose period before taking a tram to Morningside to join grandaunts and cousins for afternoon tea; or there might be a mood for walking, in which case a few of us would set out for Arthur's Seat or the Braid Hills after lunch. One Sunday afternoon was unique. 'Are you doing anything this afternoon?' a voice broke into the morning calm. Conditioned against lying easily, I hesitated, and the questioner pressed on with an invitation to accompany him to tea at a friend's house. As I knew him only inasmuch as we lodged under the same roof the eagerness of his invitation was strange. He pressed it until my curiosity was aroused, my excuses exhausted and the invitation accepted. At four o'clock we arrived, last-comers at a curious afternoon tea-party. Some two dozen people were sitting on chairs in a rough circle, most of them looking more stiff and uneasy than first-year students at one of the professional tea-parties then fashionable in university circles. Cups and saucers were being balanced with markedly different degrees of skill. The middle-aged man on my left was adept at controlling cup, saucer, plate and sandwich at once; the youth on my right, who looked much about my own age, was hot and bothered, and seemed likely to shoot tea over us both at any moment. In the grandaunts' lounge at that hour they would be talking, I recollected enviously, about Caithness friends, or Gilbert and Sullivan opera, or a recent novel or film. It was all the more startling therefore when the left-hand guest murmured in an impeccable Morningside accent that he taught in a renowned Edinburgh school for boys and was guilty of sadistic feelings when whacking his pupils. Before I could gather my wits and make some reply, the guest on the right stated that he worked in a garage out Gorgie way and often stole two shilling pieces from his mother's purse. 'Don't most people at some time?' I muttered, looking desperately round the room until caught by our hostess's watchful eye. She moved me adroitly to a chair beside the student who had lured me to this Oxford Group meeting, and who proceeded to talk about Dr Buchman and his Four Absolutes, with total waste of breath. Two Absolutes anyway, Truth and Honesty, scarcely seemed to match that afternoon's invitation! It was no way to win converts.

At a later date, three of us who were bored and exasperated by the local Oxford Group's attention decided to invite one of its prominent student members to tea in one of Princes Street's splendid teashops, professing to have a serious interest in Moral Rearmament at last. He, poor fellow, was an innocent, doing his best as he saw it. Bravely he sat for nearly an hour, changing colour frequently, while we followed each other with obscene 'confessions'. At last he broke away, saying that we would have to continue our talk at some other time. There was no other time; he became understandably adept at avoiding us, concluding no doubt that there were more promising subjects for Moral Rearmament than the three bawdy and heartless cynics who had conspired to shock him. Religion was not urgent for us. We had no great hostility towards it, except as a force which, we believed, had blighted Scottish cultural development, but which was at last fairly harmless, at least in Britain if not in Spain. There were a few churchmen such as Leslie Weatherhead and George Macleod, who were more interesting than most to listen to, but who came to Edinburgh only on rare occasions; and nothing changed when they had gone. Nothing in life was really engrossing. Academic work was a pointless game, politics either romantic unrealism or unscrupulous self-interest, sex trivial or stupidly addictive, religion the expression of self-indulgent emotionalism or cultural conservatism. Omar Khayyam was right:

> For let Philosopher and Doctor preach
> Of what they will, and what they will not—each
> Is but one link in an eternal Chain
> That none can slip, nor break, nor over-reach.

And again, with special relevance to our Scottish situation:

> Oh Thou, who didst with pitfall and with gin
> Beset the Road I was to wander in,
> Thou wilt not with Predestin'd Evil round
> Enmesh, and then impute my Fall to Sin!

> Oh Thou, who Man of baser Earth didst make,
> And ev'n with Paradise devise the Snake:
> For all the Sin the Face of wretched Man
> Is black with—Man's forgiveness give—and take!

Khayyam, as rendered by Fitzgerald, expressed it all—life was mostly a game, to be played with as much peace and enjoyment as possible. So goodbye to the University Settlement, the Student Christian Movement, the Students' Representative Council, Socialism and the lot! No fuss, no straining, no recrimination. Slip away quietly; that seemed good sense, one day. But sometimes there was a feeling of emptiness on the following day; and there was increasing reluctance to get out of bed any morning. The day began soon enough at noon. There was no urgency in time—whatever that might be. There was an apt line in Yeats's play, *The Countess Cathleen*: 'The years like great black oxen tread the world,' but I could not add honestly: 'And I am broken by their passing feet.' Slow, peaceful oxen! A water-boatman, shooting now and again here and there on the well's surface, between periods of inactivity—I felt at times like that, but certainly not broken yet, in spite of the professed tedium of life.

The situation began to change as the result of an evening in 'Macgregor's', a pub known later as 'The Charles', on whose

site the university's pharmacology building now stands. Four of
us were discussing the way in which traces of earlier cultures
may survive in unlikely circumstances. 'Look at Ross here!' said
one, 'three hundred years of Calvinism haven't obliterated traces
of Roman Catholicism!' I expostulated indignantly, but he
pressed his point. To my dismay it became evident that
ignorance on my part of the nature of Catholicism made it
impossible to argue against him. Pride was hurt by this
revelation of ignorance, for I boasted an above-average
knowledge of religious systems, and had known Roman
Catholics nearly all my life. I went back to Cowan House and
knocked on the door of a Catholic student, Sandy Hislop,
convert son of a Church of Scotland minister. 'I want to know
about your Church.' He looked startled. 'Well— what? What
exactly?' 'What it does. What it teaches.' After some hesitation
and fumbling about his room, he produced a copy of Karl
Adam's book *The Spirit of Catholicism*, and saw me out with
relief which was premature, as I returned two or three days later
with questions which, he suggested, would be better discussed
with a priest than with him. The suggestion was unwelcome.
Visits to a priest would be misunderstood by other people, who
might mistake intellectual curiosity for intention of conversion.
It appeared, however, that only fifty yards away at number 24
George Square there was a priest available. It was winter; so
there was cover of darkness for the eight o'clock appointments
which Hislop arranged, to continue once a week for an indefinite
period with no commitment on my part. The priest was an
Englishman, an austere figure in white robes and sandals who
received me in a small panelled room on the attic floor. Week
after week he talked for an hour in a dry, precise voice to a
silent listener who asked no questions, and who had made it
clear that he had no interest in attending services of any sort,
dismissing them unseen as emotional activities irrelevant to his
intellectual purpose. The talks were clear, logically constructed,
interesting; they showed that intellectually Catholicism was
worthy of respect. After six months the priest, Father Fabian
Dix, asked if he had met my requirements sufficiently.
Answering affirmatively, I thanked him and went away. It had
been enough, no more was required. Life continued as before,
marked by occasional discussion of religion or politics but
without commitment to any particular party or church. Religious

commitment did not seem necessary, or possible, until the beginning of 1937.

Two or three days before the end of the 1936–7 Christmas vacation I was busy sawing logs, alone. My grandmother had taught me to use a saw when I was little, and there was pleasure always in the rhythmic movement, especially when two of us used the crosscut, and in the sound and smell as steel worked through fresh pinewood. It was a clear frosty January day, silence broken only by the saw and by the calling of wild geese busy on the river flats, half a mile away. We were in the middle of a spell of hard bright weather. It was a joy to go out each morning, when the sun rose to touch the white bulk of Ben Wyvis with colours of pink and gold. That great table-mountain stood north-northwest, some eight or ten miles from the house, dominating the landscape and endlessly fascinating as it responded to weather changes. Sometimes it seemed remote in a purple haze; sometimes it vanished in grey cloud; it was most splendid in winter, when sheeted in heavy snow and shining in the winter sun. That morning in January the wood was smooth-grained and the saw rang without hindrance. At length I stopped to rest a few minutes, looking round appreciatively at Ben Wyvis and at the lesser hills beyond the valley, feeling at peace with the world. Suddenly my mind was flooded by awareness of God as real and present, and in the same flash there was certainty of the reality of Christ, and the fact that I must follow him in the Roman Catholic Church. After standing silent a little while I put down the saw which I had been holding, and went into the house to tell my father. He had been suffering a severe attack of influenza and was still bed.

'I've been thinking a lot recently about religion,' I began.

'Isn't that a waste of time?' he replied.

'I don't think so!'

'Well, have you come to any conclusions?'

'Yes, I think that I must change mine.' He made a grimace, 'There'll be a hell of a row if you do!'

'I suppose so,' I said, 'but I'll wear it as long as you don't mind.' He laughed.

'*I* don't mind! One bloody religion's as good as another in my opinion! Will it make any difference to your work?' I did not think so, and he asked me what next term's programme contained. We were talking about that when my stepmother brought his lunch and summoned me to mine. Nothing more was said about religion, and

next day I returned to Edinburgh and, a few days later, surprised
Father Fabian by appearing at his door. He sounded somewhat
sceptical about my intentions, especially when I repeated my
determination to avoid going to any services for the time being. He
fetched two copies of a missal, printed in parallel columns of Latin
and English, opened one and placed it in my hands. Slowly we went
through the text of the Mass; he commented with his usual clarity
and patience and, as usual, I listened in silence. Love demonstrated
by dying; Christ given to sinners, to us, for us; us given to God
through Christ, offering ourselves with Christ to God, offering to
keep the commandment to love one another as He loved us—loves
us, always. The crisp, dry voice went on. The book was closed.
'Do you believe that?'
'I think so,' was the answer.
'Enough to die for it?' There was a long pause before I
answered,
'I hope so.'
He talked then about confession and how to make a confession,
but it was difficult to pay attention to that, after thinking about
the divine love revealed in Christ's willing sacrifice which we
were invited to share. A date was agreed upon, when I would be
'received' into the Church. Two days before it I got influenza
heavily and was put into isolation by the Cowan House matron.
When visitors were allowed into my room again some came to
question my decision, about which they had heard when I was
isolated. Two agnostic friends, and a cousin training for ministry
in the Church of Scotland, came and reasoned with me quietly
and cogently. In the light of the previous two years' reading
there was nothing new in their arguments. I listened and replied
with a feeling of great peace and certainty. My two agnostic
friends promised to give any support they could, if I should run
into trouble after becoming a Catholic, and left me feeling deep
affection and gratitude towards them both. 'At any rate, we both
still accept the same Lord,' my cousin said, with his hand on
the door-knob; then smiled, and closed the door gently behind
him. At number 24 George Square, I discovered later, the
opinion prevailed that Father Fabian had probably seen the last
of me. He was agreeably surprised to receive a message asking
for a new date for the reception ceremony.
Matron agreed to allow me out on what was, although I didn't
know it at the time, Ash Wednesday, 10 February 1937. I felt

shakey from a mixture of nervousness and recent illness. My first confession must have been a strange affair as all I remember of it was anxiety that I should not faint before it was finished. In those days people with a Presbyterian background received conditional baptism when reconciled to the Catholic Church but I have no doubt that I had been validly baptised as an infant by the Free Presbyterian minister in Kilmorack. After the ceremony I went back to bed and it was not until Sunday that I attended Mass for the first time, and met a number of Catholic students afterwards.

On Wednesday evening I had written to my father, saying that I supposed the balloon would now go up, as I had been received into the Roman Catholic Church that morning. His reply arrived on Tuesday following. He had never dreamed, he wrote, that when I spoke of changing religion I was thinking of anything more than joining the Church of Scotland, or perhaps the Episcopal Church. 'As you have turned your back on your family and its tradition and have chosen to throw in your lot with reaction and superstition,' he continued, 'you will no doubt understand that you are not expected to show your face here again. I hope also that you will not continue to finance your education with money from a Protestant trust.' (The reference was to the Highlands and Islands Trust scholarship which I held.) The following post brought a letter from my stepmother, saying that she had never seen my father so distressed but that I should maintain contact with him by letter. 'Although at first he won't answer your letters, he will come round in time.'

And so I wrote three letters; the first to thank Jean, my stepmother, for her kindness; the second to the secretary of the Highlands and Islands Trust resigning my scholarship; a third, painful one to Dad, trying to explain that neither money nor a girl had motivated my action—that I had followed my conscience, as he himself maintained one should do always, at whatever cost. He did not reply. The Secretary of the Trust wrote to say that the Trustees did not think I was obliged legally to resign the scholarship but out of respect for my conscience, payment would be discontinued! Grandaunt Helen said, when she heard what I had done: 'Rome is a fashionable phase students go through,' and smiled in a kindly fashion over her teacup. Grandaunt Jean was reported to have said: 'Well, he's brainy, and of course those brainy people do odd things! Perhaps

he'll get over it. All that Latin and stuff!' My brother David, in
whom I had confided when visiting Father Fabian, said: 'I don't
understand why you're doing this, but I'll stick by you.' My
two agnostic humanist friends asked how things were going, and
whether I had enough money to see me through the term, and
although I assured them that there was no problem until the
Easter vacation one of them dropped a cheque for £20 into my
mail the following morning. One of the students from Inverness
said, 'for heaven's sake come off it! You're going round looking
as though you've seen a vision. You are not turning into a mystic
are you?' I protested weakly that I was not conscious of looking
any different from usual and offered him a drink.

I may have looked dazed for some days, not least as a result of
first experience of Mass in the Catholic Student's Chapel in
number 24 George Square. Nothing like it existed anywhere in
Scotland. Indeed the Professor of Fine Art was heard to declare
to a visiting Professor that nothing like it could be found except
in eastern Mediterranean regions. The former drawing-room on
the first floor of number 24 had been converted by Father
Fabian into something very like a Greek village church. All
daylight was excluded by thick curtains over the one, large, bow
window in which stood the main altar. The ceiling above the
altar was painted blue, spangled with stars cut from silver paper.
A backcloth of black and gold was surrounded by an elaborate
gilt frame and on the altar were two large imitation bronze
candlesticks and great vases of bronzed artificial vegetation. The
altar frontal was changed regularly to match the liturgical colour
of the day. One frontal, a favourite among students, was made
of red silk shot through with silver cupids gamboling through
sprays of silver foliage; the material had once formed part of the
curtains which graced the salon of Madame Raffalovich in Paris.
The chapel walls were hung with lengths of silk and damask in
red, blue, green and gold. There were four side altars and fifteen
sainted shrines: St Margaret of Scotland and St Giles,
represented by painted wooden cutouts, shared a place with the
major Dominican saints. There was a lot of gilded wood and
plaster, and votive lamps of various shapes, sizes and materials
hung where they could. Here and there a brace of pudgy cherubs
clung precariously to the wall, in danger of being struck to the
floor by the occupant of one of the seventy chairs available for
worshippers. 'What holds it together?' asked an awed visitor.

And one of Father Fabian's colleagues retorted, 'Faith and tintacks, helped by a little paste! Dedication? to Saints Rocoque and Baroque!' Some of the materials had been bought for a few pence in Edinburgh junk shops and some had come from friends of the Dominican community which staffed the house. There was a smell of incense in the air, varied at times by a smell of hot candle wax. It was all very different from the bare simplicity of the Free Presbyterian Church at Kilmorack, or even the Church of Scotland buildings with which I was familiar. Had it not been for the student on my right who showed me the proper places in the missal as Mass proceeded, I would have been lost completely on that first Sunday. It was not unlike the first day at school in Inverness, but for the small numbers and the strange, colourful, pagan-looking surroundings.

After Mass I was introduced to the Chaplain, to Roman Catholic students in the university, Father Giles Black, a stout red-faced dishevelled figure in rather grubby white robes, who seemed to be in perpetual motion and productive of a considerable amount of noise as he shouted greetings to one person after another in the students' common room on the floor beneath the Chapel. The Chaplaincy was staffed by three Dominican friars, I discovered. Fabian was superior, Giles chaplain to undergraduates; the third, Aelred Whitacre, was the community's official theologian. All three had seen service in the 1914–18 war; Fabian as an Anglican chaplain with the Royal Flying Corps, Giles as an ambulance driver in the French Army (he held the Croix-de-Guerre), Aelred as a Catholic chaplain in the British Army. All three were university graduates; Fabian from Cambridge, Giles from Oxford, and Aelred from Louvain. Two were English. Giles was a patriotic Scot. After school at Merchiston and student days at Oxford, he had been ordained in the Scottish Episcopal Church and had serve as a curate at St Michael's, in Hill Square, Edinburgh, then a notorious centre of 'High Church' practices. Later he served in Granton-on-Spey, where he outraged some of his Anglo-Catholic friends by providing services to suit both 'high' and 'low' tastes in worship. It was thought by his colleagues at the chaplaincy that in spite of his varied experience of life he regarded all students as innocent lambs, free from guile, who strayed only very slightly now and them from the paths of righteousness. It was not exactly so with him or them. He saw much about which he refrained from comment, believing that praise works more constructively than blame, and accordingly looking always for the good in people.

The Catholic student body was small, about 150 it was estimated, in 1934. Some of the leading figures were from Lancashire Catholic schools; many of the Scots commuted daily from places in Fife, Lothian and Stirlingshire. There was a well-known and popular black student from the United States, Joe Washington, who later became a doctor. There were few Catholics among teaching staff in the university, perhaps about a dozen, of whom the most distinguished was the professor of mathematics, Edmund Whittaker, whose reception into the Catholic Church in 1930 had shocked or angered many members of faculty. He and a young mathematics lecturer of native Lancashire Catholic origin, Dr, later Professor, W. L. Edge, were loyal supporters of the Catholic chaplaincy, in themselves living motives of credibility to young, insecure students from the Scots-Irish working class.

Although Catholic students were a relatively small group in the university, I found them varied and stimulating. They loved argument, and my combination of pacifism, socialism, and 'Home Rule for Scotland', was a standing invitation to begin, or continue, discussion. Events in Spain complicated issues greatly. As Catholics most of the students at the chaplaincy felt strong, or at least reluctant, sympathy for Franco. There were Spanish refugees in Edinburgh who gave accounts of Republican atrocities, among them one unhappy man whose ideology was socialist but whose humanity had been outraged by what he had seen, to such an extent that he was struggling with a growing feeling that he would have to throw in his lot with Franco, which he did eventually, joining the Nationalist army. The political background of the majority of Catholic students was probably radical , but they were made uneasy by Communism and Popular Fronts. The old archbishop of St Andrews and Edinburgh, Andrew Joseph Macdonald, spoke frequently and vehemently about Russia and the 'Communist menace'. 'Atheistic Communism' was denounced by Pope Pius XI. The three priests at 24 George Square were politically conservative, willing to listen and to argue patiently, but plainly unable to understand why someone like myself could not see the rightness of their position. They were handicapped in discussion by the fact that in the Dominican monthly magazine, *Blackfriars*, some of their own brethren, especially Gerald Vann and Victor White, were commenting on current affairs from a radical Christian standpoint. There were others like them, in France and Germany, for example the German Dominican, Franziskus Stratmann, who wrote a book welcomed by pacifists, published in English as *The Church and War* (Sheed & Ward 1928). The Edinburgh Dominicans were distressed by reports of cruelty, were opposed to anti-semitism and encouraged joint meetings of Catholic and Jewish students, but on the whole they stood as it were paralysed in a political no-man's-land between contending forces which they hoped would quieten down somehow or go away.

They were at ease with the Senior President of the Catholic Society, a girl from an old Scottish Catholic family in the northeast, who studied medicine and was a prominent member of the students' Conservative Association. Kitty, solidly upstanding in good tweed, was kind, always courteous, and steady in religion, work, and politics; the type of conservative who deplored bad housing, unemployment and poor educational opportunities, but hoped that patient reform would straighten out society without much disturbance of its basic structure. For such as her, privilege and possessions—of which her family had little in proportion to its ancestry—implied a duty of stewardship and concern for those whom God had placed in a less fortunate station in life than their own. Good nature, kindliness, tolerance, and an early habit of authority, made her an obvious choice for leadership posts in student society. Firm leaders were needed in the chair at Catholic student meetings which were often bedevilled by protracted wrangling between barrack-room lawyers bred in school debates, and charged with much energy from the surge of their own voices. Even a witty antiquarian talk by Father Fabian on something as harmless as 'Old English Inn Signs', would be followed by a legalistic verbal avalanche under the title of 'Any other business'. 'Madam President! On a point of order!' 'On a point of information!' 'I beg to move that this meeting adjourn!' 'I move a direct negative!' On it went, until simple hunger for chips induced a general desire to close the meeting, or until there was no longer a quorum. Father Giles sat through it all with a patience admired, but not envied, by his brethren.

There was poverty among those students, shown sometimes
in poor physique and an unhealthy pallor unknown in Cowan
House, in quality of clothes, in the pieces which they brought
in for lunch, travelling daily from mining towns and villages by
train or bus. The chaplaincy was a place in which to make tea,
to play table-tennis, or cards, to shelter in between classes, a
place for lounging and gossiping, for getting advice and
sometimes financial help, for praying, together or quietly alone
in the flickering light of votive lamps and candles in the chapel.
It struck me one day how many of the students were remarkably
matter-of-fact about prayer. An attractive, intelligent girl standing
in a talkative group glanced at her watch, said, 'Well! I must be
off and say some prayers,' and skipped out of the commonroom.
A boy might say, casually, 'I'm going up to the chapel for a few
minutes. See you when I come down?' They tended to rattle
through public prayers, for example the daily recitation of the
Rosary at noon. I had no trouble with the idea of fingering
beads, as a means of helping concentration, but could see little
point in rattling through breathless repetition of phrases, even if
some of them did come from the Bible. Plainly, however, I was
odd man out in this.

Answers to prayers were expected, and announced. That was
not something new in my experience of older people, but it was
new to find so many girls and boys of my own age with
confidence in the power of prayer. Gradually, as knowledge of
family struggles and sacrifices increased, it became clear how
central prayer was in the lives of some of the students, even
although it appeared to be so mechanically conventional at times.
A little over a year had passed before my reserve of scepticism
was jolted by an experience during a walking holiday. Two of us
had decided to explore Perthshire, with a tent, for a few days in
the Easter vacation in 1938. My companion was a third-year
medical student, native of Edinburgh, Catholic by birth. We
found ourselves trudging along an empty road one afternoon, in
heavy, endless rain. About three-thirty I remarked gloomily that
we were in a hopelessly wretched state and would have trouble
finding a camp site. The clouds were clasping the hills tightly
and low, and the rain had settled in for the night in a way only
too familiar from much experience. 'We'll just have to pray for
it to stop,' said my companion, drawing rosary beads from his
pocket. I refrained from saying 'Huh!' audibly, and joined in

meekly, surveying the landscape with cynical eye. Five decades of beads went through my companion's fingers; there was no change in the weather. He launched into the prayer, 'Hail, holy Queen, Mother of mercy!' and we rounded a corner, passed a house with drawn blinds and lights on, and walked along the edge of a plantation. The rain stopped. We pitched our tent in the lee of the wood, and had just finished doing so when the rain came down again. 'We should say the Rosary in thanksgiving,' said my companion; and so we did. Next morning the sun shone. 'Where were you in that awful night?' asked a shopkeeper later in the day. When we described our camping spot he exclaimed: 'Good heavens! Yon was the gamekeeper's house you camped near. Nobody's ever allowed to camp in that glen; and you wouldn't have, if the storm hadn't kept him in!' My friend grinned at me as we left, from a superior height. He was taller than me anyway.

17

There was much to learn; much was strange, in spite of previous instruction. It was strange how other students seemed to pop in to St Francis' church, or the Sacred Heart church in Lauriston, or the chaplaincy itself, to make confession. They could be seen kneeling in preparation, sometimes so long that one wondered what on earth they had done. Confession seemed to do very little for me. My moral behaviour hardly seemed to change; it was very ordinary; of course I should work harder, and often intended to do so. Somehow it did not happen. Of course I drank too much at times; but I did no harm to anybody when I was drunk—just went to sleep or was sick in suitable places. There appeared to be little point in often repeating my litany of spinelessness before God and man in the confessional, when it was so obvious to everyone who knew me, but I went to confession occasionally as a special way of acknowledging God and my dependence as a weak willed, time wasting gift wasting creature, on His goodness and mercy. He would show what way I should go; in the meantime there was plenty to occupy time and energy until I got some firmer pattern into my life. I would resolve to get up for Mass daily at 8.15; and then reduce that to once a week, with equal lack of success. Sunday Mass and the Sunday afternoon service of Benediction was the limit of my achievement. But there was a closer link than before between religion and daily life, through the fact of involvement with the chaplaincy community of priests and students for whom so much was integrated already by faith, hope, and love.

It felt right to be where I was, and much was oddly familiar even in the heavily decorated chapel and its furnishings. The colours, the clouds of incense, the seven-branched candlesticks brought out for Benediction, the vestments worn by the priests, the plainsong rendered by Dr Edge's small male-voice choir, were indeed all unfamiliar in earlier direct experience but all in various ways wakened lively echoes of The Old Testament. The Mass was full of it—the sprinkling with hyssop in the Asperges at the beginning, the references to Melchizedek and Abraham, to the Lamb of God, many things, bringing together Covenant and Passover and Calvary in one great prayer of thanksgiving, which not only looked backward through history but forward to the fulfilment of the last great vision of St John. It was as though fragments of coloured glass in a kaleidescope were falling into brilliant patterns, as I tried to explain to a Free Presbyterian cousin from Skye. The words, actions, colours, shapes, even the smells directed one towards God. 'H'm-m!' he said thoughtfully, 'but how can you stomach the Roman Church's scandalous history?' By then I had learned much more about its scandalous history than he had ever done. I had read the historian Edward Gibbon, and also Lord Macaulay's famous account of a New Zealander standing amid the ruins of London far in the future and musing on the phenomenon of papal survival. I drew comparisons between the Old Testament Church and the Catholic Church, between patriarchs, prophets and high priests on the one hand, and kings, visionaries and popes on the other. I analysed the genealogies of Christ offered in the gospels of Matthew and Luke, with their record of murder, incest, adultery and infidelity among the People of God as it moved towards its messianic fulfilment. The trouble with the Protestant churches, I declared, was that they had turned to schism in a perfectionist zeal, subtly asserting their own righteousness in place of Christ's. One of the best reasons for joining the Catholic Church, I maintained with a sudden feeling of fresh understanding, was precisely the obvious fact that above any other it is the church of sinners, depending upon Christ alone as the source of that holiness exemplified in its saints, in people like Francis of Assisi or Father Damien of Molokai, or in Mary and Joseph. The fruits of the Spirit, and the scandals, are always there, as Christ said they would be. As he passed me the last chocolate éclair—we were having tea in 'Medical Martin's' at the corner of Forrest Road—my cousin observed, 'Well, I still don't see why you had to go over to Rome; but you seem to have the root of the matter in you yet!'

At that stage I was not reading the Bible much, not nearly as much as I had done in earlier years, and nothing remotely like as much as I would do again in the future. The realization that a People of God must have existed before the Book which we knew, had shifted the focus of my attention to the People and its traditions. Wherever one looked, at whatever text or translation of Scripture, there was no perfect original manuscript to study, but only later, much later, copies, issued with the authority of councils of rabbis, or Christian leaders of one sort or another. Father Fabian had pointed out how interpretation of biblical texts was influenced by the secular knowledge of particular periods; sometimes, as he remarked, more affected in fact by ignorance than by knowledge. And so my dominant interest through the year immediately after Ash Wednesday of 1937 lay in members of the Church, their worship, discussion of ideas, reading, recreation, hopes and fears. They were the People to whom I believed myself led; and they made me feel at home better than they knew. There was little feeling of a break with the past, in spite of the doors now closed to me in Inverness-shire; it was rather as though I had found a place to which I belonged truly. A pass had opened into a new land to which many clues had been leading in my earlier years; and in that land one scene after another rapidly became familiar.

The approach of the Easter vacation raised a problem. Cowan House closed for the vacation. My father's attitude was unchanged. Although he did not destroy my letters to him but put them into a pocket unopened, to be read when he was alone, I could not go home yet; so Jean, my stepmother, reported.

What, then, could I do for four weeks? An answer came through
Sandy Hislop, in the shape of an invitation from his parents to
stay in the manse at Ardwell, in Wigtonshire. His father, Dr
David Hislop, had gone into semi-retirement as Church of
Scotland minister of Ardwell and Sandhead, after many years in
North Morningside. He was what might be called a 'High
Church' Presbyterian, who commonly wore a black cassock and
a silver pectoral cross of Celtic design as an expression of his
belief that he was the lawful *episcopos*, the bishop, of his
parish. He firmly believed that the Church of Scotland was the
true *Ecclesia Scoticana*, the authentic descendant of Columba
and the Ionan tradition, from which Scotland had been diverted
by Queen Margaret and her sons in the eleventh and twelfth
centuries. Reaction against Roman abuses however had gone too
far at the Reformation, especially in efforts to simplify worship,
and particularly sacramental worship. Like his friends, the Rev
Dr George Macleod of Govan, and Principal Macgregor of
Trinity College, Glasgow, he believed strongly that Holy
Communion should be celebrated at least every Sunday. He
recognized the Roman Church as one branch of the Catholic
Church and was glad to see that it had mended its ways, at least
in some places if not everywhere. When his elder son showed an
attraction to Rome he discussed the matter with him quietly and,
convinced of his seriousness and honest conscience, suggested
that he might support him in a hall of residence in order to
avoid any awkwardness which could arise from continuing to
live in an Edinburgh manse. So Sandy had lived in Cowan
House during term time, going home once a week with his
washing, until his father's declining health suggested the wisdom
of seeking a light country charge. Ardwell and Sandhead had
become available, particularly attractive as Mrs Hislop's family
belonged to Stranraer, where an unmarried sister, Dorothy
Aitken still lived, within easy driving distance of Ardwell.

The weeks at Ardwell were idyllic. There was much sunshine
that spring, glancing off the fresh early grass after a shower and,
towards evening, bathing the low green hills in an unearthly light
as the westward sky filled slowly with gold. David and Frances
Hislop were firm but gentle people with a gift of hospitality.
The manse was light; there were hyacinths in bloom, their smell
competing with bowls of pot-pourri; and everywhere the air was
fresh. Nothing was hurried; the eyes and the movements of

David and Frances were peaceful, their voices quiet but expressive. Everyone was occupied, including Sandy and his younger brother, Jock aged sixteen, who was being treated for a trace of tuberculosis. I slipped gratefully into the manse life. There was a wealth of books. Every morning after breakfast I settled comfortably in a small study, to translate a compendium of mission statistics from French into English. Unfortunately for the translation I discovered Thomas Carlyle's epic *The French Revolution* and was hypnotised by his prose and the vivid intensity of the story, until every line of the two stout volumes bound in red and gold had been read, and read again. Then came *Heroes and Hero Worship*; and stimulating comment by my host. For lighter reading there were volumes of essays by E. V. Lucas and others. There was no thought of the examinations which lay ahead.

During the weeks at Ardwell I got to know Sandy Hislop well. We shared a room and talked across it from our beds night after night. I had thought him prickly and stand-offish when we first met in Cowan House. It is almost an understatement to say indeed that we disliked each other cordially at first meeting. I judged him bad tempered and boorish, and he regarded me as a tiresome pup. He had been crippled seriously by polio at the age of twelve and wore a surgical boot. Medical opinion suggested he would have a short life, dying probably in his mid-thirties. As small boys, we discovered, we both had dreamed of becoming farmers one day. He loved cattle and would have bred Aberdeen-Angus bulls. Although I shared his admiration for the breed, and for Clydesdale horses, he found it a little difficult to match my interest in the growth of oats and potatoes; but he was a better judge of cattle than I was of crops. In our night-time talking he dropped his customary shyness and allowed the sensitive, imaginative side of his nature to appear. It was a surprise to discover a strain of sentimental romanticism behind that brusque front, and tinging a passionate love of Scotland. One night, munching a hunk of cake which he had fetched from the kitchen about two o'clock, he expressed a fervent hope that before dying he might have some years as a priest in the Dominican Order. He would regret not having children, he said, and as he enlarged on that I thought of Charles Lamb's essay, *Dream Children*, and had no words of reply. It was perhaps as a result of confidences at night that we developed an ability to walk or read in companionable silence for hours at a time during the day. The greatest friendship in my life was beginning in the quiet of Ardwell manse, almost imperceptibly.

On Saturdays we travelled into Stranraer by bus and stayed over the weekend with Sandy's aunt, in order to attend Mass on Sunday. Miss Aitken was firmly Protestant and in her will set aside a sum of money to ensure that Sandy's boots were all that they should be while he lived, but making sure it could not be touched by the Roman Church or the Dominican Order which he had entered. Her manners were impeccable, and her kindness was unfailing. We chuckled affectionately over some of her old-fashioned spinsterish ways, as we thought them, especially the locking-up routine at bedtime, with rolling up of carpets in front of fires and careful checking of every window lock. In letters home I remarked on how much she and my grandaunts had in common, and I wondered privately what were my father's feelings on learning that I was enjoying the generous charity of members of my mother's church. In those days I said few formal prayers but had a sense of God's presence much of the time; I felt that the peace of Christ was in that house.

18

The following term was dominated by threatening financial problems. It was my last term on a Cowan House scholarship. There would be lodgings to find and pay for in the 1937–38 session. There was the question also of how to get through the approaching summer vacation, without the work opportunities available at home. Other students were anxious to find work, and at length twenty-two of us were engaged to pick raspberries on a fruit farm near Blairgowrie. We were to live in three bell tents. There was a cookhouse built of corrugated zinc, with a six-foot-long hot plate over a coal fire. Our cook failed to arrive and I was nominated for the job, with a guaranteed wage of one shilling and sixpence a day from each of the other members of

the party and a sum, also per head, for catering. The farm
supplied milk and potatoes in abundance, but the cook had to
buy anything else in the town, for breakfast, lunch and an
evening meal. There was long argument with one member of
the party, a colonial student, who offered to rustle sheep and
poultry and was loudly angry when his idea was quashed. The
weather was good, and by noon each day the heat in the
cookhouse was productive of rivers of sweat and an intense thirst
slaked by innumerable cups of tea. The need to save money and
the attraction of lying down after a long day's work (7 am to 7
pm), ruled out much participation in the camp's routine evening
visits to Blairgowrie bars and the socialising with local girls
which was part of the programme. There was another camp not
far away, of young miners from Fife who sang all day as they
worked among the berries, and who addressed each other as
'Sir', but there was no contact of any kind between the two
camps. The miners probably were saving also in that time of
depression, were perhaps more careful with their money than
most students, and seemed less interested in picking up local
girls.

When berry picking was finished three of us set off on a
walking holiday, northwards to Braemar, then through the
Lairig Ghru to Aviemore, back over Cairngorm, down Glen
Avon to Corgarff and thence to Ballater, making use mainly of
Youth Hostels, although that meant walking over twenty-four
miles on some days. One night was spent in the legendary
Maggie Gruar's house in Inverey where climbers were at home,
the fire was bright, food was plentiful and good, the charges
modest, and our hostess worth a journey in her own right. She
seemed old to us, and perhaps she was in body but certainly not
in wit and intelligence and ability to assess character. Another
night was in cold contrast, five bodies under the Shelter Stone
at the head of Glen Avon while wind and rain blustered outside
until morning. No porridge there, only miserable cornflakes and
lukewarm tea, and three bars of chocolate on the march, until
our rumbling stomachs were brought to the hostel at Corgarff
with its store of tomato soup, tinned beans and wrapped bread.
Had Glen Avon been the world's most beautiful valley we would
have been unaware of it, consciousness of empty stomachs and
weary bodies dominating all else. The Blairgowrie work had
been preparation for a month in Morar, in the west of

Inverness-shire. It had seemed a good idea to spend at least part of the summer in one of the traditionally solid Catholic areas of Scotland. An old barn would be cheap and sufficient shelter, and some other students might be attracted to share it, given Morar's assets of sea and mountains, river and loch, and the proximity of Mallaig with its harbour and pubs. A letter to the parish priest, Canon John MacNeil, brought the reply that barns were rare but that there was one on the north side of the bay, at a place called Buorblach, which might be had for a shilling a night. 'It is not much,' he wrote, 'but I know of nothing else. If you think it might do, write to Mr John Gillies.' I thought it might do, and two other students agreed to share it for the first fortnight.

Those who have travelled to Morar or Mallaig by train from Edinburgh in the early morning, will know the feeling of arrival in another world. There were Gaelic voices greeting friends in English; a bustling official was calling to someone in Gaelic; the July air was soft and warm and fragrant, and a gentle rain fell steadily, dripping from the fuchsia bells beside the track. Everything dripped. Then, in mid-afternoon, the rain stopped. The sun shone, the world sparkled. To the west the islands of Eigg and Rhum became visible. By that time we had slithered and splashed along the shore to Buorblach, following a shortcut available when the tide was out, an alternative to a longer path along the hillside but requiring gumboots or agility if we were to reach firm ground with dry feet. Bruce and Gordon and I reached it, squelching a little. The barn was a dry-stone building, with a platform of hay at one end, bare earth at the other; bedroom and kitchen, as someone remarked. Here and there the rain dripped through, but nowhere too inconveniently. The wind, we would discover, had more entry than the rain but that too was no hardship, especially when sleeping bags were dug into the hay. The primus stove was soon alight, and I was detailed to go up to the croft house in search of milk. A young woman came to the door and, as I spoke, a voice called from inside in Gaelic, 'Who is there?' 'A lad who is asking for milk,' was the answer. 'What sort of lad?' My Gaelic was enough for me to call out in the same tongue 'A good lad!' and there came to the door an elderly woman with outstretched hand and a warm smile, her eyes bright with friendliness as she drew me by the hand into the house. There are no adequate words to express the warmth of hospitality which marked that house at Buorblach, a second home to me and to many others. Mrs Gillies was a widow with a son, John, nicknamed 'Foxy', and a daughter, Morag—the one who had answered my knock—and two foster-sons, Walter and Noel. If she had a fault, people said, it was that she was too kind, 'too soft with the young ones.' I did not think so, being a young one myself in that lively, warm place where laughter and quarrels went easily together and strangers were quickly made welcome.

The house had the usual Catholic emblems, but nothing which appeared distinctively Gaelic. French and Italian repository art and styles of devotion had taken over in Morar very effectively by 1937. On the other hand there was a little more awareness of local Catholic history than there was in Beauly. This was not surprising, since in the eighteenth century there had been a small illegal training centre in Morar for apprentice priests. It was first established in 1712 on an island in Loch Morar, Eilean Ban, in a turf and wattle house destroyed by government forces after the Jacobite rising of 1745. Re-founded later it changed location several times and was even briefly at Buorblach itself, probably on the site of the Gillies' house. Eventually, in 1829, the West Highland seminary was united with a similar one in the east to form St Mary's College, Blairs, near Aberdeen. The Morar people were aware of this history and proud that their country had been known as 'Blessed Morar', the heart of the old religion in the West Highlands. A vestment and a chalice from penal times, when the practice of their religion had been proscribed by law, were kept in the chapel. The chalice bears a name and a date inscribed in Latin within the base—'*Vincentius Marianus*', of the Order of Preachers, '1658'. Nobody, not even the well-informed parish priest, could give any further information about that seventeenth century Dominican friar.

On our first evening, after the rain, we went to call on Canon MacNeil. We were shown into a book-lined study and asked to wait for a few minutes. My companions, both non-Catholics, examined the shelves, uttering occasionally exclamations of surprise as they discovered evidence of acquaintances with ancient and modern literature in several languages. John MacNeil, from the Hebridean island of Berneray, had arrived at Blairs in his thirteenth or fourteenth year so ill at ease with the English language that he was given *Treasure Island* to read on his first day. Blairs and the Scots College in Spain, at Valladolid, had extended his education. After the 1914–18 war, in which he had a distinguished record as a chaplain with the Highland Brigade, he was appointed parish priest in Morar, where he was to remain until his death in 1958. He served for many years on the Inverness-shire County Council where, it was said, he was the only man who could keep Lovat and Lochiel, the chiefs of the Fraser and Cameron clans, in order. We knew none of this as we scanned his books with envy and admiration, increasingly prepared for the impression made when he entered the room, a tall, gracious person who put us immediately at ease, and who tactfully rescued anyone who got out of his depth during conversation.

The first Sunday in Morar was fascinating. It was a hot day, the loch glassy, beside whose north west corner the Church of Our Lady and St Cumin stands. People stood outside the church talking. More arrived on foot or by car. A boat came down the loch with the people from Meoble, far east on the south side. On every side there was an air of reunion, an animation more marked than anything outside the chapel in Beauly and totally unlike the subdued atmosphere in which people greeted each other outside the Free Presbyterian church in Kilmorack. Men smoked. There was laughter, before and after Mass. The chapel was packed. A small choir sang at intervals. People told their beads and pored over prayer books while Mass went on, Hilaire Belloc's 'blessed mutter', broken by the prescribed bells at the consecration and communion points and by a clear, thoughtfully constructed, five-minute sermon. A few people had gone to confession before Mass began. Frequent confession it appeared was not common even in 'blessed Morar', no more than in Beauly where even people who attended Mass daily went to confession and received communion only twice a year. Frequent or daily communion was rare. Morar people did not seem specially holy. Not many received communion that Sunday, but there was contentment on the faces of the congregation as people came out from the chapel into the hot sun. I had followed Mass in a Latin/English Sunday missal, distracted sometimes by the choir, and by curiosity about what my neighbours were doing, and struggling to fix my attention firmly on the liturgy. Prayer, whether liturgical or private, seemed mainly a constant struggle to centre wandering thoughts on God. It was easier in the evening, at the service of Benediction where there was much to hold and focus one's senses; the white circle of the Host in a jewelled monstrance, surrounded by bright clusters of candles; clouds of incense in the air; music and bells, and the attention of a congregation gathered not by obligation but, for the most part, from simple choice. Not that Sunday obligation seemed to weigh very heavily on people who for centuries had been accustomed to irregular opportunities of attending Mass. 'There's an awful lot to be done in the summer, when there's visitors,' someone remarked one day, 'but we can always make up in winter what we've missed in summer. But I wouldn't want to miss my morning and night prayers, though I'll sometimes be up a wee while in the morning before I say them!' Someone added, 'I don't suppose the night prayers are all that good when there's been a ceilidh, and you've had a bit too many drams!' 'You speak for yourself!' he was told amid laughter, for he was known as a merry drinker, and a faithful Catholic.

And so the days went by rapidly in Morar, a considerable time spent lazily on the sands and in the sea. The Central Bar was a favourite stopping place when we walked into Mallaig. There was one crazy occasion when, for a bet, I topped numerous drams and pints of beer with a quart of cider. Someone eventually gave the three of us a lift back to Morar on the back of a lorry. The tide was out, and I leaped wildly from tussock to tussock of grass between the residual pools, kilt flying as incredibly I retained my balance until the Buorblach shore was reached; then up the hillside and into the barn, where the hay rose to welcome me, as I collapsed into it and passed out. There was a party later that night in the barn, one of several during our stay, livened by songs and stories and much laughter, with Johnny and Morag and other local young people joining us. One weekend we ran out of money except for a few shillings which the others wished to spend entirely on cigarettes, being sure that postal orders would come on Monday. Fortunately, we were invited to supper on Saturday by Miss Mackellaig of the Morar Hotel, and to lunch on Sunday by Dr Rutherford, the mother of an Edinburgh student, on holiday with her family. After buying oatmeal therefore, to ensure porridge for breakfast over the next three days, the rest of the money was spent on cigarettes. We did not have to pay for milk; it was given freely by Mrs Gillies, in accordance with Highland custom.

One other student came to share the barn, a keen politician
called Robert MacIntyre, who took a prominent part in political
debates in the University Union. We argued for hours about the
best way of advancing socialism in Britain. I maintained that the
weight of English conservatism would continue to dominate
Scottish radicalism, as it had done for over two centuries, and
therefore every effort should be made to secure self-government
for Scotland. Given that, there would be soon a socialist
democracy in North Britain to show the way ahead to the other
parts of the British Isles! Scottish independence, nothing else,
should be our goal. He was convinced at length, but I did not
foresee that he would be the first Scottish Nationalist Member
of Parliament at Westminster, and for many years chairman of
the party. 'Indeed!' comments a contemporary member of the
SNP with no use for Dr MacIntyre, 'And that was how you
committed mortal sin in Morar!'

The people of Morar peninsula were not greatly interested in
possibilities of Scottish independence, in 1937. Like most
Highlanders they were liberal in outlook, but attached to
personalities more than to parties, and slow to change their
allegiance once they had elected a Member to Parliament. The
County Council in Inverness was more significant than
Westminster in their lives. Religion had little connection with
politics, and Gaelic culture even less. There were still one or
two old people who were monoglot Gaels, notably one ancient
lady who had lived nearly all her life far up Loch Nevis and
whose English was even less than my Gaelic, being restricted to
three remarks about the weather which involved a vocabulary of
six words. First impressions at the station were easily
exaggerated. Morar had little native knowlege of Iain Lom, or
Alasdair MacMhaighstir Alasdair, or of *Carmina Gadelica*. The
Gillies family, and others like them, were interested in hearing
others talk about the great tradition but retained little of it
themselves except wisps and receding echoes. It was faintly
recalled by occasional wireless programmes, by reports of the
Mod, and by a thin line of singers promoted by the annual
National Mod, only some few of whom were untouched by the
Celtic twilight of Marjorie Kennedy Fraser. A few Gaelic songs
were learned in school, but Morar was already far in decline as a
Highland community, both culturally and economically. At one
time part of the Clanranald lands it had been involved heavily in

Jacobite rebellion, but there seemed to be little spirit of rebellion left. After all, there were few people left in the land, probably less than one thousand of all ages between Mallaig and Arisaig.

After Morar, a very different resting-place was offered in that long vacation of 1937. Sandy Hislop had gone on a pilgrimage to Lourdes, a year earlier, in thanksgiving for the gift of faith. Most of the journey was by sea to Bordeaux; he was very sick. By the time the ship entered the Bay of Biscay the weather had improved; he struggled on deck in search of sun and fresh air, flopped into a deck chair feeling weak and wretched, miserably alone because he knew nobody on board. As he lay, with eyes closed, a compassionate voice said, 'You look shattered!' He looked up, to see a big, stout, red-faced man with a small ginger moustache and ginger hair who introduced himself as George Taverner. George was accompanied on the pilgrimage by his two unmarried sisters, Millie and Suey. All three were familiar with Lourdes. They adopted Sandy effectively for the duration of the pilgrimage, and afterwards he went to visit them in their home. They invited us to stay with them for a fortnight, after I left Morar. And so I came to the mining village of Whiterigg, a few miles from the town of Airdrie, in industrial Lanarkshire; from one island of Catholic tradition to another very different in outward appearance, but rooted anciently in the same Gaelic culture and a history of coolness towards London governments.

Whiterigg has been demolished, its people rehoused in the village of Plains, and elsewhere. It was a mining square of small, dark brick houses opening out in front to a road, and at the back to a central muddy yard with lines of middens and outdoor lavatories. There was a small recreation hall; a small general store kept by an ex-miner, one of whose legs had been crushed by a rock-fall; a policeman's house; and, on a ridge above the village, a primary school which served also as a chapel, the priest's house beside it. The Taverners' house, at one time occupied by a mine manager, was on the other side of the village on slightly rising ground. It was a rambling one storey affair; thin brick walls plastered over; jerry-built and chilly; cracked here and there by subsidence caused by old mine workings; behind it mounds and hollows where men had delved in search of coal during the great strike of 1926. The country immediately around looked bleak and empty, after the wild beauty of the Morar peninsula. If Morar was in decline, Whiterigg was worse,

since everyone except priest, teachers, policeman and grocer was
unemployed. There was better food in Morar, more of it than in
Whiterigg. The difference showed in people's complexion and
physique. There was some work in the Highland village and at
least a prospect of more, if the fishing industry developed in
Mallaig and tourism, forestry, and home industries in the area
generally. In the Lanarkshire village the future closed when the
pits closed, and the only thing for a sensible person to do was to
leave it as soon as possible.

Millie and Suey Taverner taught in the school. The Taverners
were a mixture of Irish, Welsh and English, the Irish strain
predominant. George had a London University external degree
in Arts, some experience of journalism, and of life in America.
He had been married; but his wife had died, childless, after a
short life together. He had settled with his sisters, looking after
a piece of garden and some poultry, repairing the house
endlessly, sweeping chimneys, caring for the dogs (two lively
black Labradors), reading, writing odd fragments of prose and
verse, and maintaining a wide circle of friends, in the
neighbourhood and in Glasgow, in Catholic circles especially.
He opened doors which might otherwise not even have been
pointed out, and greatly advanced our education.

The Taverner sisters were short and plump, cardiac
complexioned, bright eyes and spectacled. They walked together
arm in arm, perfectly in step, sensibly dressed, down through
the village briskly, then more slowly up the hill to the school-
chapel, to teach or to worship. One of them played the
harmonium at Mass and Benediction while the other kept the
children in order; children sat in rows near the front, older
people in rows behind them. When school was over for the day,
or a service ended, the sisters went down the hill together and
through the village once more, their daily passage the most
familiar and regular feature of village life. There were smiles for
people at their doors, and words in passing; but rarely a break
in the rhythm so expressive of family union. At home they
knitted and cooked, the latter activity shared by their brother.
Shopping was on Saturdays usually, in Airdrie, more rarely in
Glasgow. Some of what they bought was distributed quietly in
the village by means of the children, as a result presumably of
discussions in their bedroom at night; they avoided discussing
other people's needs openly. They entertained generously and

without fuss, showing an old-fashioned assurance that men should be fed to bursting with meat and vegetables at least twice daily and sustained through the inevitable intervals between meals with tea or coffee, scones, biscuits, fruit cake, shortbread, and other delicacies to tempt a hesitant appetite. They ate moderately themselves, with enjoyment of food but with greater pleasure in promoting other people's enjoyment of it. Moderation was a keynote of their lives. They were moderate in speech. When their brother and his friends passed hours in heated argument they listened, sometimes with obvious amusement, and for the most part kept their own counsel. They cared deeply about the children in the school, and sometimes when men were deep in discussion of current affairs, in the sittingroom, they would sit in the kitchen talking over some family's difficulties. For them teaching was a God-given vocation, to which they were totally committed. By example and exhortation, and a judicious use of the tawse, they did their best to make law-abiding citizens and good Catholic Christians out of the children of Whiterigg; Boyles, Devlins, Maguires, MacMahons, and others, descendants of starving Irish immigrants in the previous century.

Days at Whiterigg went by quickly. Sandy and I shared a room; our comfortable sleep was broken each morning by the dogs, let in by George at eight o'clock and leaping on to our beds, wet tongues busy on our faces, insisting that we get up. Breakfast, preceded always by grace, was a vast leisurely meal, after which there was no fixed programme until the main meal of the day about 5.30 in the evening. Some days we went to Glasgow, calling perhaps on the editor of the *Scottish Catholic Herald*, or on one of the professional families with whom George was friendly. We rode usually on a tramcar, from Airdrie to Glasgow's George Square, as trams were more frequent than buses, and cheaper at twopence each way for the whole or any part of a journey between Airdrie and Paisley. As the tram rattled and swayed through the open country between Coatbridge and Shettleston, George maintained a flow of largely inaudible words, though increasingly thick clouds of smoke from his pipe—and my irritation increased correspondingly for I disliked his tobacco, and disliked even more attempts to keep up conversation at the pitch of one's voice and in public places, especially on religious subjects. Political topics were almost as embarrassing, and George's jokes were often worse! He considered it part of his Catholic duty to cultivate a Rabelaisian humour. Good bawdy jokes and verse were part of his social equipment, the verse frequently composed by himself. He maintained that this was in line not only with ancient Catholic tradition but also with Scottish working-class tradition, which had defied successfully the heavy attempts to suppress it made by clergy of many denominations. Although willing to accept his argument in principle, I felt that he forgot sometimes that in Scottish tradition at least there was a recognition of time and place for bawdry which might exclude the upper and lower decks of a Glasgow Corporation tramcar.

A more comfortable place for George's humour was the pub on the border of Airdrie and Coatbridge where we used to meet local friends, notably an unemployed miner, Joe McGlone. Joe was at home with economics and politics. He and George had a deep interest in Irish history, especially the struggle to achieve independence. They were part of the radical movement represented by the Independent Labour Party and deeply concerned to work out some kind of synthesis of their politics and their religion. Joe read anything he could lay his hands on that was relevant to that problem, and brought an acute intelligence to bear upon it. His knowledge of papal encyclicals was extensive, respectful, but critical; he had clear views as to the limits of infallibility. While grateful for Pope Leo XIII's *Rerum Novarum*, (issued by the Catholic Truth Society as *The Workers' Charter*), he saw it as a beginning of recognition of working-class rights, as a document which increased rather than diminished his own personal responsibility as a Christian and as a worker. He was interested therefore in what had been happening elsewhere, for example the rise of Cardijn's 'Young Christian Worker' movement in Belgium and France; Pope Pius XI's 'Catholic Action' movement, which was intended to make everyone into an apostle in their own environment, Young Christian Workers, Young Christian Students, and so on; Don Luigi Sturzo's 'Popular Party' in Italy and its failure to halt Mussolini. George had a Chestertonian romanticism, something of a twopenny-coloured Belloc-derived dream of The Middle Ages, the 'Age of Faith'; but Joe was much more realistic, more involved in immediate problems of unemployment and poverty, and in the struggle of large Catholic families to survive the double burden of unemployment and membership of a religious minority which currently experienced open and covert hostility from bigots.

Discussion came back, again and again, to the matter of private property, and how we should regard papal and episcopal emphasis on 'the right to private property'. George was attracted by Distribution and, while admitting the impractical nature of Chesterton's 'two acres and a cow', and the Distributist 'back to the land' experiments generally, was hopeful that distribution of wealth might be achieved satisfactorily through profit-sharing, co-operatives, or perhaps social credit unions. George possessed, and studied, the *Summa Theologica* of Aquinas, in the English translation published in 1912, by Burns Oates and Washbourne. He was encouraged by Aquinas's insistence on the common good, and on the priority of common need over the accumulation of surplus wealth by individuals. But, in practice did that mean socialism? Was the study of Aquinas turning him into a Marxist, as one of his respected priest-acquaintances maintained? Was Marxism really as incompatible with Christianity as Pope Pius XI seemed to think? The Soviet constitution looked as though it might work well, if freed from hostility towards religion; surely a Christian communism was possible and desirable, capable of attainment by peaceful democratic methods, through education of the people, by slow reform rather than sudden revolution.

Might this not be possible in Scotland? Unlike Russia, with its history of absolutism, Scotland cherished a long democratic tradition, or so it was claimed. There were doubts about that. I knew that John Knox had scorned the idea of popular voting and that there had been scant democracy in Scotland in the three centuries following the Reformation. We were all familiar with the Protestant Action Society's bigotry and understood the fear, widespread in the Catholic community, that self-government in Scotland would be marked by discrimination against Catholics. The General Assembly of the Church of Scotland, and Professor Dewar Gibb of Glasgow University, attempted to camouflage religious bigotry under anti-Irish Polemic. George could quote the report, approved by the Assembly of 1923, in which unity of race was listed as a quality which brought God's special approval upon a nation; the title given the report was *The Menace of the Irish Race to our Scottish Nationality*. My father, despite his socialism, his dislike of racialism, and his low opinion of the Church of Scotland, had given it grudging approval.

Joe, with a wife and family to support and with close personal knowledge of industrial conditions, was always more involved in economic and political analysis than George was at any time. The latter was perhaps the more inclined to believe in the inevitability of violent revolution as a means of necessary structural change. Joe was less optimistic about the effectiveness of such change as a means of transforming the quality of life. The struggle to create a classless society would fail unless jealous selfishness gave way to self-sacrificing love of other people. I could see no reason to be confident that the contemporary class struggle would be followed by a lasting synthesis, instead of by a new class system. The dialectic seemed eternal. The dispossessed would become possessors of wealth and power and a new body of dispossessed be created. The wheel would go round, and nothing change significantly, unless the hearts of men and women changed and became truthful and loving. Black shirts, brown shirts, red shirts, cricket shirts; they covered types of Imperialism abroad and exploitation at home, varieties and degrees of violence, and could be exchanged easily enough, with little or no change in the wearers. Mussolini was an example; at one time a socialist regarded favourably both by left-wing politicians, and by English railway enthusiasts, before acquisition of power revealed his true character.

George would raise the question; whether the rise of Fascism could have been halted by the 'Popular Party' in Italy, if the latter had countered violence with force instead of with words. Had the *Partito Populare* been led by a dynamic layman, instead of by an idealist priest, could it not have saved Italy? When such questions were raised pacifist views were soon under attack, as surely as when I faced the university Socialist Society, though in somewhat quieter tones. There were no easy answers in Whiterigg and Coatbridge when religion and politics were brought together. Sometimes Catholic students from Glasgow University, from working-class families, joined in our discussions, primed with economic theory or political science; but never anyone from the village.

What we shared with the people in the village was Sunday Mass and Benediction; hot bodies, frequently in damp clothes, packed together in uncomfortable positions; hymns of questionable theological soundness, accompanied by Millie on the harmonium; rosary prayers said at astonishing speed; short

intervals of silence opened and closed by bells; squeezing up
and down a narrow passage-way during the giving and receiving
of Communion. The way of prayer associated with the use of
rosary beads is intended to be meditative, a series of short
meditations on the life and work of Christ, from the archangel
Gabriel's announcement of his coming, through the principal
events of the Incarnation to the great fulfilment which we call
Heaven. During recitation of the rosary, the imagination forms
a picture on which attention is concentrated by the person
praying. Concentration is helped by regular passage of beads
through the fingers and by a background, a sort of ground bass
almost, of vocal prayers, chiefly the 'Hail Mary'. Thought and
feeling are directed towards Jesus, with or without precise
petitions, for essentially the rosary is an aid to private, personal
prayer of a contemplative kind. This was probably not unknown
to many of the people of Whiterigg, but the Sunday public
recitations were rather different—the 'rapid rosary' instead of
the 'slow rosary' of private devotion. The phrases of the 'Hail
Mary' and the 'Our Father' rose and fell, hammered or rattled
out with a hypnotically regular beat, at amazing speed, as though
the members of the congregation dared not let up for fear of
losing their hold on what they were doing; prayer fences taken
at the gallop!

19

Sometime later that autumn, I do not remember when exactly,
Father Fabian took me to Walsingham, in Norfolk, a remarkable
contrast to Whiterigg, and a happy introduction to the ancient
Catholic tradition of England. In autumn 1937 the Slipper
Chapel and a small Priest's House stood alone in the fields about
one and a half miles from the village. We stayed in the village
and walked out each morning through a quiet hedge-enclosed
lane to the tiny medieval Slipper Chapel, where Father Fabian
said Mass, and I learned to serve as acolyte. Each morning after

Mass we said the Rosary slowly in front of the statue of Our
Lady of Walsingham, seated in her medieval English dress with
the Christ Child on her lap. Then we walked back to the village,
Fabian in his white Dominican robes, the fresh morning dappled
green and gold under a blue sky, and nobody was put out by the
sight of a friar in an English country lane or village street. An
idyllic week flew by, an unforgettable entry into that England of
which I had read in Arthur Mee's writing, a place of life-rich
hedges, golden wheatfields truly edged with scarlet poppies, flint
churches with brick manors of great beauty, quiet villages with
centuries old cottages and houses, where even the public houses
were relaxed and peaceful. Never before had I been in a place
like the lounge bar of the Black Lion Inn, where two village
worthies sat each evening discussing local affairs while absorbing
two, and never more than two, pints of beer each. The sisters
who kept the Black Lion served roast beef, and home-made
apple or blackberry tarts with real cream, and pastry
unsurpassable in excellence. At Whiterigg, George had
introduced me to the work of Belloc and Chesterton with a
somewhat tiresome enthusiasm which, I suggested sarcastically,
sprang perhaps from the English strain in his blood. After that
week in Norfolk I felt more in sympathy with Belloc's feeling
for England and read appreciatively one evening some verses by
Arthur Quiller-Couch which began something like this:

O quiet heart of England, like a psalm
of green days, telling with a quiet beat!

At Walsingham I prayed for reconciliation with my father and
a welcome back home. It was the first time when I could say
truthfully that I was asking Our Lady's help with some
conviction in my heart.

Intellectually I had given assent to the Church's teaching
about Mary's place in the communion of saints, but it had left
me emotionally unmoved. Then, one night, I dreamed that I
was looking at a picture of her. All that I remember of the
picture now is that the predominant colour was blue, and that
the face was very beautiful and peaceful. In the morning a feeling
of peace remained with me; I began gradually to feel more at
home in the Lady Chapels of Catholic churches after that. At
Walsingham I thought about the home of Nazareth and
something of the peace that must have been there.

At Walsingham also I found a way of praying with rosary beads which was satisfactory. Before beginning one of the fifteen 'mysteries', the thing to do was to recollect where possible a relevant passage of the Bible, for example the account of the Annunciation in the second chapter of Luke's gospel, and then to form a picture in one's imagination. With imagination focused on the picture, fingers on the beads, one began to meditate on the scene and the words of the passage while reciting the vocal prayers, the 'Our Father', and 'Hail Mary' slowly. Sometimes attention simply rested in the scene contemplated. At other times some prayer of adoration, or thanksgiving, or petition might form in one's mind and heart; a prayer, for example, echoing Mary's 'Be it done to me according to Thy word!' or, when contemplating the mystery of the Crucifixion, 'God, be merciful to me, a sinner'; contemplating the Resurrection, 'My Lord and my God!' So I learned a new way of prayer at Walsingham and asked for reconciliation with home, and also for some indications of what I should do with my life, for I had no clear idea myself.

Two academic sessions were to follow before I came to a tentative decision about the future and my memory of the sequences in life during that time is chronologically unclear. It was time to leave Cowan House and three of us moved into rooms in number 18 Buccleuch Place, with two unmarried sisters as our landladies, the Misses Pringle, whose father had been a doctor and who found it necessary to supplement their income by 'taking in young gentlemen'. The momentous decision to do so had been made two years or so before we three moved from Cowan House. In a flat below the Misses Pringle lived Dr Sophie Weisse, the old teacher of Sir Donald Tovey, then Reid Professor of Music in the University. Through Miss Weisse, Sir Donald was asked if he knew any suitable young gentlemen; he did, and after that the good sisters never needed to ask again, or to advertise, for there was always a waiting-list of students keen to become their lodgers. T. V. Hughson, W. J. S. McKinnell and I moved in together, Tom Hughson occupying a single room and Bill McKinnell and I sharing a huge room with an Adam fireplace and two large windows overlooking the Meadows, one of Edinburgh's large well-planted open spaces.

To live 'care of Pringle' was good fortune for anyone, but for me, financially reduced, as my Cowan House scholarship had come to an end, it was an immense help. For twenty-seven shillings and ninepence a week the Pringle sisters provided a cooked breakfast, lunch, high tea, milk and biscuits for bedtime, a coal fire, and laundry. Their purpose was not to make a profit but only to make ends meet and to ensure, as far as they could, that their 'young gentlemen' were happy. The elder sister, Helen, whom we addressed as Miss Pringle, referred to us always as 'young gentlemen', but the younger sister, Miss Clemmy, referred to us as 'boys' sometimes. She took care of the cooking and the laundry, while her sister kept the accounts, as she had 'been in business'.

The accounts were a delicate matter. No money or cheques ever passed from hand to hand. On one morning each week envelopes appeared beside our breakfast plates, with statements enclosed. Into them we put our cash, or cheques, and they returned at a later meal with duly receipted statements inside. The statements varied according to whether we had missed meals, or had entertained guests. There were modest charges for guests, who might be invited to any meal, even breakfast; there was a modest deduction if, after giving notice in advance, one of us was out for meal. The sisters' idea of justice was astonishing; their housekeeping equally so since they fed us remarkably well though not, of course, on the lavish scale to which we had been accustomed in hall.

Miss Pringle's appearance was incredible, for surely no thinner person ever existed. She was an articulated skeleton covered with dry membrane, so devoid of flesh that it seemed she might rattle if shaken. Usually she wore long black dresses and long earrings; she had a way of pressing the tips of her bony fingers together and agitating her head as she made a point, until you feared some part of her would drop off. Pursing her thin lips and shaking her head more than usual she asked one day in her customary precise dry tones if she and Miss Clemmy could speak with me privately. I accompanied her into their kitchen-livingroom. Miss Pringle coughed a few times; Miss Clemmy looking very grave while the throat-clearing went on. At last Miss Pringle spoke.

'It is Sunday evening, Mr Ross. My sister and I are most put out!'

I was puzzled; there was usually on Sunday evenings a meeting of members of the Student Pacifist Association in the room Bill and I shared, but it was always very quiet, and one of us kept watch at the door to let our friends in without ringing the bell.

'I am sorry, Miss Pringle; I didn't realise we were making a noise which might disturb you.'

'Oh, no! no! You are so quiet and well-behaved—we have no complaints about noise.'

'But, then—I don't understand!' Miss Pringle tapped her fingers together and her head shook until it seemed the earrings must fly across the room;

'So many people, Mr. Ross! What will the neighbours think?'

'But we never meet any neighbours on the stairs, or hardly ever. Have they complained?'

'Oh, no!' said Miss Clemmy, 'but they must see at least from their windows all those people coming and going.'

'Yes!' agreed Miss Helen, 'most embarrassing! What *will* the neighbours think is going on in this building!' The reason for their agitation occurred to me suddenly; they feared that the neighbours would think that a brothel operated at number 18. There was one not far away, it was believed; in the same street.

'I understand, Miss Pringle. We hadn't realised what the neighbours might think! I am very sorry, and we will meet somewhere else!' So our only disagreement was amicably settled.

Miss Clemmy was a total contrast to her sister, plump and rosy complexioned, motherly by nature and in figure. It was she who called us in the mornings, for breakfast at eight o'clock. One of our predecessors described how she had entered one morning and, moving swiftly and quietly through an atmosphere of whisky and tobacco, had opened both windows wide. 'I am sorry, Miss Pringle,' he ventured to say, 'I am afraid I drank rather much last night and I don't feel like breakfast!' 'Of course! That is quite alright,' she answered gravely; 'My dear father always said that young gentlemen must learn through their mistakes how to deal with their wine. Would you like me to bring you some coffee now, or later?'

Miss Clemmy loved music and would comment occasionally on the records which we played, after lunch most days. One afternoon I was listening to a gavotte by Bach, and remembering that I had left a book in the dining room went to fetch it. Miss Clemmy had cleared away our lunch dishes and was dancing alone beside the table, her apron held out in front of her and a dreamy smile on her face. She gave me a broader smile and remarked, as she picked up a loaded tray: 'That music! So beautiful! I simply had to dance.'

There was a Pringle brother who lived also in the flat, occupying a small room off the dining room, and not much in evidence; a thin, grey, unsteady old man with a pipe, whom we glimpsed now and then when the kitchen door was ajar, sitting with a newspaper by the fire. Every afternoon he went out, returning punctually for tea until one day the sisters came to my room and pointed out a photograph in the evening paper about an unidentified elderly man having died suddenly in the street. Their brother had not returned and they feared that it was he who had died; they would be grateful if I would go to the mortuary and find out. It was strange to see him lying there with no look of shock or pain on his face, and to realise that until he died I had not known his proper name and had never before looked at him so long and attentively. It struck me how indifferent to his existence we had been, and I felt guilty as I left the mortuary.

Life at number Buccleuch Place was comfortable and we all got on well together. I had stopped going to lectures except those in Church History, at New College, where I was the only Roman Catholic student. Fitful gestures towards making a study programme and keeping to it did little to disturb a state of academic drift. Breakfast in pyjamas and dressing-gown was a leisurely introduction to morning papers. The first engagement of the day was a meeting for coffee somewhere, at 11 a.m., continuing until lunchtime. The second standard engagement was somewhere at 4 p.m. for tea, continuing for an hour or more. In the evening there might be a concert, a debate, some society meeting, the cinema or theatre, a gathering before or after in someone's room, coffee and tobacco maybe until morning, solemn and hilarious talk, much bantering wit, and an underlying anxiety pushing through when someone remembered final examinations, and the greater problem of what to do after them for the remainder of our lives.

Early in December 1937 my stepmother wrote to say that I might come home for the vacation on condition that religion was not to be discussed at all. It was agreed accordingly that I should return in time for Hogmanay. It was almost a year since we had all been together and my father was out when I arrived, just in time for the evening meal. Granny greeted me with both hands on mine, but no words. As we gathered round the table she looked at me and her lip trembled. In Dad's absence it fell to me as a rule to say grace at meals. My stepmother was looking at the table. I said the usual grace, and my grandmother's face cleared; we sat down relaxed. As we were finishing the meal, Dad came in, said 'Hullo! So you got here!' and took his place; the conversation turned to weather and farming as though there had been no break in family relationships. That night when Granny was going to bed I asked whether I might come and read the Bible to her as usual. There was puzzlement in her eyes but she accepted the offer, and her only comment was: 'You are clipping the words in an English style!' as I closed the Gaelic New Testament. There was no discussion then, or ever, of why I had gone 'over to Rome'; no quarrel with her about religion.

It was not just as simple with my stepmother. Jean was indignant at the thought of anyone leaving the house without breakfast, even on a Sunday morning. In those days Catholics were required to fast from midnight if they proposed to receive Communion, abstaining completely from food and drink. Free Presbyterians had fasting customs but none as severe as that and Jean was horrified that anyone should walk the mile to chapel on an empty stomach. 'Not even a cup of tea?' In spite of our discussion on Saturday, bacon and egg appeared on Sunday morning; an apology for returning it to the oven was met with an indignant snort and 'I never heard such nonsense!' but the following Sunday passed without incident. Fortunately Jean did not learn that when kneeling before Mass, that first Sunday, I fainted.

There was little unpleasantness from anyone. A large drunk man planted himself squarely in front of me on the pavement one Saturday afternoon and asked if the 'bloody Protestant church' wasn't good enough for me that I had to 'turn to effing Rome'. The Free Presbyterian minister had preached about my fall one Sunday, and Dad had walked out of the church; but there was no attempt to get in touch with me, although the minister stared hard one day, passing slowly, as always, in his car. 'I am sorry to hear you have joined the Romans,' said 'Holy Sandy', the lay preacher who stood in for the minister on alternate Sundays, cycling past slowly on the Beauly road. 'Yes,' I replied; and there was no further conversation. Old Mrs Macdonald, at one of the Barnyards small holdings, who had maintained always that I would be a minister, stared thoughtfully as she acknowledged 'Good morning!' but asked no question nor offered any comment. At home the vacation went by quickly and peacefully. In the

village I was welcome in Miss Fraser's house, and at 'Lochletter'
in Croyard Road, where Willie Fraser, youngest of the four
'Kilty' brothers, and his mother, became firm friends.

20

In the university terms, during sessions 1937–38 and 1938–39,
four areas held my interest, represented by the Catholic Students
Union, the Students' Pacifist Association, the Scottish
Literature Society, and the Union Debating Hall.

In the Catholic Students Union there was an urge to activity
along new lines. We approached other student societies with
proposals for joint meetings, which were accepted usually,
notably by the Jewish Society and by Congregationalist and
Church of Scotland students. Meetings with the last two raised
slightly awkward questions about hymns and prayers. Holy
Mother Church frowned upon *communicatio in sacris*, the
sharing of sacred things. It was feared that 'indifferentism'
would be encouraged if we acknowledged a common
Christianity. Vital distinctions would be blurred. The matter
was referred to Archbishop Macdonald, who ruled that we might
sing together hymns which were in common use among both
parties; which would not, therefore, raise theological difficulties,
for example 'Praise to the Holiest in the height'. We might recite
also the Lord's Prayer, although when we did so there was some
obvious fumbling and mumbling about 'who' and 'which',
'debts' and 'trespasses'; and a Catholic silence as our separated
brethren acknowledged 'the kingdom, the power, and the glory,
now and forever. Amen.' In this small way we moved
unknowingly towards the Second Vatican Council, and the
modern ecumenical situation.

Another advance resulted from the conviction, among some
of us, that we needed to read and study seriously in order to
take a responsible place in the church, in the modern world.
The head of the Dominican Order in Britain was approached

and agreed to donate £150 so that a library might be started for the benefit of students, with the single reservation that books bought with the money should be considered Dominican property. Shelves were provided in the commonroom of number 24 George Square, to hold the 300 or more volumes which we could buy at that time, with so much money. The publishing firm of Sheed and Ward did much to meet our ideas, with series like the Ark Library which included Karl Adam's *Spirit of Catholicism* and Christopher Dawson's *Progress and Religion*. We bought as much of Jacques Maritain's writing as could be found in translation; Eric Gill, E. I. Watkin; Stratmann's *The Church and War*; Martindale's *The Mind of the Missal*, and much else; Romano Guardini, Martin D'Arcy, Goodier, Arendzen, Vincent McNabb; the Catholic Evidence Guild's volume of training outlines; Berdyaev also, for we intended to be up to date in Edinburgh, and he was read among the more enterprising students in other churches. Henri Gheon, Chesterton and Belloc provided lighter material; the first represented by his lives of saints, for example *The Secret of the Curé d'Ars*, for we were not unmindful of traditional piety. Butler's *Lives of the Saints*, edited and revised by the erudite Herbert Thurston, S. J., was accompanied by some other reference works, mainly dictionaries—the *Shorter Oxford Dictionary*, Lewis and Short's *Latin Dictionary*, and Larousse.

We were eager to begin a branch of the Catholic Evidence Guild and to provide speakers at the Mound to proclaim the Catholic Faith. The proposal was drowned firmly at birth by our chaplains, whose attitude was supported by the Archbishop. Instructions were, to keep away from the Mound, no matter what Protestant Action speakers might be saying. The Archbishop was determined to dissuade us from any involvement in sectarian controversy. No matter if Catholic chaplains and students were libelled again and again by Protestant demagogues. We must keep the peace, and console ourselves with the words of Matthew's gospel: 'Blessed are you when men revile you and persecute you and utter all kinds of evil against you falsely on my account. Rejoice and be glad, for your reward is great in heaven, for so men persecuted the prophets who were before you.'

I was involved once or twice by the Honorary Secretary of the Scottish Catholic Truth Society, the late John Barry, in talks or discussions of an uncertainly ecumenical nature. On one such occasion the subject for discussion was 'The Marks of the Church'. As a recent convert from Presbyterianism I arrived, Bible in hand of course, to be greeted testily by an Episcopalian curate with the words 'Good heavens! Surely the subject is too deep for that!' The evening was a strain upon everyone's good intentions, the slight comfort being that Mr Barry was satisfied with my performance in it. We were not trying to find common ground but to win arguments, to score points against each other in order to impress doubtful or fainthearted listeners. Or so it seems in retrospect.

The Students' Pacifist Association was a kenspeckle group of some sixty members, including four or five Catholics. There was an impressively consistent girl, Eleanor White, whose position had been shaped by the Society of Friends, but the rest of us were in search of a position which we could maintain and present as intellectually and practically viable. Some members were not as definite as that. They were worried by the evil of war and came to examine pacifism, in faint hope that it might offer an effective alternative to military conflict. They pressed their doubts upon us within the association's own meetings, which usually took the form of seminars. Outside the association, challenge seemed endless. Although some people professed scepticism about the imminence of a general war, most were worried by the violent evil which existed then in Europe and was threatening to spread farther. In spite of the Peace Pledge, the majority of people were pessimistic about the effectiveness of non-violent resistance to tyranny, and known pacifists were drawn into endless discussion which often became heatedly abusive, not least when members of the Socialist Society were involved.

Some part of Pacifist Association problems rose from deep suspicion of certain elements in the peace movement. This came to a head in connection with the Scottish Peace Congress held in the Usher Hall in 1938 and taken over completely by the Communist Party, with the intention of whipping up support for a military alliance with Russia against Germany. As a delegate from the University Catholic Students' Union I watched with dismay as several hundred people were manipulated skilfully by three men on the platform, Professors Gordon Childe and J. B. S. Haldane, and Krishna Menon. Who

more suitable to chair a Scottish peace conference than an
eccentric looking, world-famous professor of Prehistoric
Archaeology? Gordon Childe was voted into the position with
no difficulty. The rows of Scottish Trade Union members were
overawed by academic distinction on the platform into robotic
endorsement of anything that the three wise men proposed. A
procession of approved speakers was summoned from the floor
to the platform while delegates from units in the peace
movement grew increasingly uneasy and worried-looking. The
Professor of Prehistoric Archaeology eventually nodded benignly
towards me and granted two minutes speaking time. I quoted
Lenin, and suggested a dilemma to the delegates. If the Russian
government was truly Leninist, it was lying to the West when it
claimed to have none but peaceful intentions. If it spoke
truthfully to the West, why did it continue to commend Lenin
to its own people and not renounce at least some of his views,
about international violent revolution? I suggested that neither
Stalin nor Hitler could be trusted when they talked of peace.
Each in the long term had violent designs on the world. The
peace movement had to beware of wolves pretending to be sheep.
Those working for peace must not become pawns in a power
struggle between dictators. The chairman's bell rang. The
pacifist minority applauded loudly as I stepped down; the
majority sat still and silent. There was a hurried consultation on
the platform, and then Haldane and Menon moved angrily into
speech, the latter stooping to personalities and innuendo which
I was not allowed to answer. It was my first experience of the
way in which the apparatus of democracy can be abused when
clever demagogues treat subservient masses to a pre-arranged
programme of speakers, and to floods of impassioned rhetoric in
which half-truths and untruths sweep along unchecked—too fast
indeed to allow critical examination.

Soon there were other matters to think about, then Haldane's
emotionalism and Krishna Menon's spite, when tribunals were
set up to examine conscientious objectors with a view to
identifying those who were 'genuine' and those trying simply to
avoid conscription. We had campaigned for recognition of
conscientious objection to military service, and for safeguards
against any repetition of the inhuman torment of objectors which
had taken place in the first half of the 1914–18 war. Several of
us listened to tribunals in action, in order that we would all

know what to expect when our turn came. We developed a strong sympathy for Jehovah's Witnesses as we listened to the intellectual bullying to which they were subjected on many occasions. Often the Witnesses were not very bright and were easily tied up in logical knots by tribunal members, who then concluded, erroneously, that he whose logic is at fault cannot be sincere in conscience. The term 'ego-trip' was not then current or we might have applied it to the behaviour of some of those judges of other people's consciences. Most of the Witnesses were allowed some form of alternative service, having been grilled first. It became clear that most of our members would settle probably for medical service or agricultural work in the event of war.

Getting enough people together to form the Scottish Literature Society was an easier matter than struggling with questions of peace and war. Since coming to Edinburgh I had grown more and more attached to Scots literary tradition and especially to the late medieval poets, Henryson, Douglas and Dunbar. James Macpherson was displaced by Allan Ramsay and Robert Fergusson. James Hogg's *Memoirs and Confessions of a Justified Sinner* was discovered in Cowan House Library one Sunday afternoon and led to absorption in *Noctes Ambrosianae*, bought in four volumes from a secondhand bookstall for a few pence. Grierson's lectures, and Harvey Wood's course on Scottish literature, were reinforced by the knowledge and enthusiasm of other students, particularly Stuart Hood and George Davie. The former could talk with authority about Scottish novelists particularly, and the latter about the Scottish Latin poets in *Delitiae Poetarum Scotorum*, of whom I had heard, but whose poems I had not read.

Meetings were held as a rule in an upstairs room in the Meadow Bar, where we sat with our drinks round a huge table, the speakers for the evening placed at the end farthest from the door. It was a very drab setting then, a typical spare room in a typical Scottish pub, with no concessions to comfort or art; but appropriate to the tradition of Fergusson and Burns, as we conceived it then. Members of university staff, for example Dr George Kitchin, were content to talk to us there. But for such speakers as Professor W. J. Watson, on Gaelic poetry, and Dr Mary P. Ramsay, on 'Calvinism and Art' or 'Walter Scott's Sources', another drab but more respectable setting was found in the Associated Societies' hall, in the basement of Old College. That was the scene of a most disappointing evening, when Hugh MacDiarmid came to talk.

Time came, but no speaker. The audience was a bit better than usual, about thirty in all, including some formidable women, Mary Ramsay, Helen Cruickshank, Mary Dott, and Nannie K. Wells. The first we knew, but not the others, the last of whom looked ready for battle of some kind. The speaker came at last, his eyes focussing with some effort. I had only met him sober, before; a quiet, thoughtful man he had seemed then, very unlike the aggressive character who subjected us now to a rambling tirade. Edwin Muir was denounced as Scotland's greatest villain and traitor. There were passages of what sounded uncomfortably like Celtic racialism jumbled together with unconvincing linguistic theories. Sentences got lost. Names were thrown out, as unchallengeable authority for whatever it was that the speaker was trying to say at that moment. We watched one of Scotland's greatest poets struggling painfully and embarrassingly, and longed for the conclusion of the meeting. As most of us present that evening learned only later, he was going through at the time one of the deeply unhappy periods in his life. Not many people in his situation would have broken up an evening with congenial drinking companions, in order to talk to a handful of students, on a wet night, in a dingy room. From the chair I could see the anxious faces of the four ladies, in the front row of the audience, who had come to support him with their friendship, not for the first or the last time. It was a sad evening, but the most memorable in the society's experience. MacDiarmid was trying to put across passionately and drunkenly something that mattered to him more than any subject had done, to even the best of previous speakers. Language and literature were important to personal and national life, not toys to play with in academic games, or in private entertainment.

'Surely you are being narrowly nationalistic in your emphasis on Scottish literature!' was a common suggestion, tiresomely often repeated, as though we were rejecting all the rest of the world by our plea for the recognition of what Scotland had produced, and was producing again in our time. My friends and I were not asking for a literary garden in which a hedge of thistles enclosed a heather moor, with a small white rose shining in a rocky corner, and nothing else there. We saw our critics as narrow, who refused any place to thistle or heather or the 'little white rose of Scotland.' We saw ourselves as at once national and international in outlook.

The same was true in politics. I dreamed of a north-western European federation of democratic nation states, each similar to Holland or Switzerland in its internal structure, but all co-operating closely in matters of education, economy, and foreign policy. The University Union debating hall was packed usually for political debates, and offered a good forum for presentation of ideas. Three political groups were strong: Conservatives, Socialists, and Liberals, in that order. Royal speeches were prepared and debated on party lines, with care to reflect the machinery and formality of Parliament, and bringing forward burning topics of the day. I found myself critical of all, and at ease in none, for they seemed to have their eyes on the ends of the earth, or at least on London, and to show little practical concern for what took place in Scotland. At last the most useful policy appeared to be to set up a Scottish National Party and Calum Maclean from Raasay, and myself, sat with about forty others one evening on the cross benches. There was a Conservative 'government' in power, thrown out, after a lively evening, by the combined weight of Socialists and Nationalists; the Liberals abstained on that occasion, I seem to remember.

It was agreed that for the next Parliamentary Debate there would be a Socialist-Scottish Nationalist coalition, for which we would prepare together the 'King's Speech'. There was to be no such collaboration. The Socialist Society prepared the speech unilaterally, flattering me with the posts of 'Prime Minister' and 'Minister for the Highlands'. I refused the whole package, on behalf of the Nationalists; slammed into all British political parties and their deals; and declared that we were not to be used as tame lackeys by any part. 'Oh, man! This is a black day,' sighed Calum, as we sat firmly on our benches during the division. 'Indeed it is!' I replied, 'but those English stooges must learn to deal with us seriously and honestly!' The Socialists, left alone, were defeated. Could looks have killed, I would have died that night, when they heard the result. We took political debates very seriously, not only because older politicians were interested in that which we said and how we voted, but because very many among us, of whatever party, were concerned passionately about securing peace and with the abolition of poverty and unemployment—both more grim then than they have been since, for hundreds of thousands of people, who knew no National Health Service, nor Social Security.

It seemed clear to some of us that there must be closer contact between electors and elected than was possible in centralised modern states like Great Britain and France, if democracy was to survive. Large states must be broken up. In this way Scotland and Wales would be freed from control by the English majority at Westminster, free to follow their own socialist ideals. Mineral resources would be nationalised, land use controlled (with emphasis on afforestation, tourism, and hydro-electric development), Scots and Gaelic language and literature would be given an assured place in schools. We saw no reason why the Scottish people should not know three or four languages, looking to other small countries in Europe for encouragement of our polyglot ideal. A vast programme of public works would provide roads and harbours where communities needed them, for example in the isles, and would replace our notorious slums with new housing schemes equipped with the amenities scandalously absent in places like Niddrie and Craigmillar. Privately I speculated about possibilities of importing Dutch expertise, to direct land reclamation projects which would facilitate agricultural expansion, and publicly advocated massive development of market gardening and fruit-growing under glass. There was exciting scope for builders of a new Scotland, if only we were free from London—if only the Scottish people could see where their real future lay, and tear themselves away from a union which profited only a minority, and then at the expense of integrity.

21

A visit to France in the summer of 1938 stimulated these and other ideas. A postgraduate French student, Joseph Lajugie, spent a year in Scotland studying the coal industry with a view to a doctorate thesis for the University of Bordeaux. He was a practising Catholic, with great gifts of humour and intelligence, and had become a popular member of the chaplaincy congregation. He was also one of a group who enjoyed the generous hospitality of the McGinness family in Pitt Street, widowed father and three exuberant and witty daughters, with whom we played bridge or Monopoly often far into the morning. My atrociously 'psychic' bridge playing used to drive Joe to loud protests, equally incoherent in French and English. Nevertheless, overlooking atrocious bridge playing, he invited me to spend a month of the summer of 1938 at his home in Perigord, in the village of Tocane St Apre. A friend of Father Fabian agreed to cover travelling expenses. It was suggested that after two weeks in Paris I should go to Tocane, but on second thoughts it appeared more sensible to go first to the village and there improve my knowledge of the French language. In the event, six weeks slipped past in Tocane and I saw Paris for the first time many years after.

My arrival in Tocane was mildly sensational. Having missed a train connection at Perigueux I took a taxi for the last twenty-three kilometres and swept up to the station entrance in Tocane just as the welcoming party, wondering what had happened to its Scottish visitor, was leaving slowly. So there was much exclamation, and good-natured laughter at my expense, and an immediate feeling of being at home with the Lajugie family. Not only Joe and his mother had come to the station but an aunt, and some cousins, all smiling and welcoming. So began six weeks of laughter, sunshine, and friendship – the best since childhood.

Religion mattered little, it seemed, in Tocane. A big church dominated the village square but very few people entered its dull chill interior, even on Sunday. Then some elderly women, sombrely dressed, emphasised the absence of the rest of Tocane's population of 1,700 souls. Apart from Joe and me there was only one young man there, a precise fellow of an emphatically bourgeois type, totally outside the lively adolescent group with which I bathed most afternoons and danced during many evenings in a kind of village beer hall known as 'the Casino'. They professed no interest in religion but some of them displayed strong dislike, or even declared hatred, of the parish priest; two or three eventually expressed some curiosity as to why I was a 'believer'. Joe and I received communion regularly

at Mass. It was explained by one of his aunts that Joe took
religion very seriously, since his recovery from massive injuries
suffered in a train disaster, while my behaviour was quite
understandable, as all '*les Anglais*' were very strict, even when
they were not converts. It was strange to find oneself in such a
tiny minority in what I had imagined to be a Catholic Christian
land.

Apart from Joe, and two friends of his who were Socialists
and unbelievers, nobody in Tocane had even heard of the French
writers whose works were available in the Edinburgh chaplaincy.
Tocane was pagan, materialistic, pragmatic, and friendly towards
a Scottish visitor, distinguishing the land of 'Marie Stuart' from
England, admiring my kilt, and curious about life in such a
northern region. But it was with a schoolmaster, René Delfaud,
and especially his charming and intelligent wife, that
conversation would turn to politics, philosophy, or literature. Joe
lent me two novels by Mauriac which were not available then in
English, *Le Baiser au Lépreux* and *Genitrix*, which Madame
Delfaud discussed patiently, as the four of us sauntered along
quiet county roads in the evening. The Delfauds had heard of
Jacques Maritain, but had read none of his books. Étienne
Gilson was totally unknown to them. To me Baudelaire,
Rimbaud and Verlaine were simply names of unread poets. So
we extended each other's knowledge in a blissful summer in
which it was easy to forget Hitler and Mussolini, although less
easy to forget Stalin. France was secure, as viewed from the
green-gold banks of the Dordogne. René argued with me about
pacifism, as Joe did now and then, with slightly amused
tolerance. Given the French Army, and the Maginot Line, there
was no anxiety, even although Hitler was growing bolder, even
although most of his tanks might prove to be real and not merely
the plywood dummies which some people supposed them to be.
In the house, and under the big plane tree in the garden where
we ate most meals except breakfast, Joe's mother was a serene,
quietly humorous, infinitely kind and generous presence. Her
husband had been killed years before, crushed by a runaway
waggon. Joe had escaped death narrowly in the train crash, and
over many subsequent months surgeons had performed
operation after operation, to put him together successfully. She
came through loss and anxiety with strengthened faith in God,
and compassion for other people. Her house was simple and

uncluttered; managed efficiently, without fuss; beds comfortable and made fragrant by dried herbs; food unpretentious, but always good. Had Chesterton known her, he would have hailed her in some poem or essay as a symbol of Catholic France at its best. It was good to be in her company, and her face and movement remain vivid in memory.

Joe and I went with the Delfauds to Bidart, a small seaside town between Biarritz and St Jean de Luz, in the Basque country, for ten days. He suggested a weekend visit to Lourdes, and there we arrived one Saturday to find the town bursting with an estimated 60,000 French pilgrims, a noisy, bewildering national pilgrimage flood of humanity. There were no empty beds in Lourdes, everyone said, but we discovered one at least in a small attic room in a *pension* high up on the town's rim. The heat was intense under the roof; the one bed too narrow for two people to sleep there in comfort, but we thought we might pass a reasonable night lying back to back—until the first contingent of undernourished fleas moved into action encouraged perhaps by the sweat which shortly poured off us. We rose very early, exhausted by the night's unlooked-for penance, went to Mass and took the first train back to Bidart. A day visit by car to Roncesvaux, followed by a struggle to read *Le Chanson de Roland* in the original medieval French, was a more pleasant experience. Roncesvaux on its cliff was quiet and beautiful, seeming almost as restful as it may have been when St Dominic went there on pilgrimage early in the thirteenth century.

There were three parish events in which I was involved, each of which illustrated the religious poverty of Tocane. The first was the parish priest's tea-party, to which Madame Lajugie, Joe and I, were invited. It was an uncomfortable, bleak occasion, on which a dozen or two widows and spinsters, dressed in black or other sombre unworldly garments, sat in a circle on upright chairs in a large, faded, slightly musty room. There was no housekeeper, as there would have been in Scotland or England; the parish priest, in black soutane, presided over lukewarm tea and little cakes. The occasion was sad. It left an impression of terrible isolation, of one man alone in an old empty house, denied communication with other people except on a superficial level.

The annual outing for the altar boys and the 'Children of

Mary' was a happier event. I forget where we went, a few small boys with mothers or aunts or big sisters in a hired charabanc. It was a cheerful little crowd, and the priest also was cheerful. It was very like the annual Sunday School outing, from Beauly to Rosemarkie in the Black Isle by train, which I had enjoyed as a small boy. There was one surprising moment, when the driver asked if anyone wished 'to look for mushrooms' and the passengers shouted gaily: '*Oui, oui. Cherchons les champignons!*' The bus stopped. Everyone got out, and the women and girls scampered into a wood, while the males turned their backs to the wood and piddled cheerfully in a line on the opposite side of the road. French lack of embarrassment about natural functions was surprising at first, as was the mixed bathing which we enjoyed so merrily under the watchful eyes of a line of mothers and aunts sitting on the riverbank.

The third event was a parish 'pilgrimage' to a small local shrine of some ancient, shadowy saint (or perhaps it was a monument of Marian devotion). There was a straggling procession of perhaps fifty or sixty people, with desultory singing, and a short Benediction service at the shrine. It was pathetic maintenance of exhausted tradition, but the afternoon was fine and the relaxed amble along a country road was pleasant enough. The priest was grateful that we were there. We were giving a trifle of time, from an agreeable flow of activity, but would be away soon, absorbed in university life once more. Meanwhile we played bridge, bathed in the river, danced, picked chanterelles, gathered snails after a day of rain, ate and drank and talked, and were almost as distant from him as everyone else was—black crow on a bicycle, at whose passing seventeen-year-old Roger spat ostentatiously.

22

About six months later I was in Dublin, as a member of an Edinburgh University debating team, taking part in an international debate with American, English, Irish and Scottish students. A few weeks later many of us were in the Cambridge University Union, on a similar ploy, and comparing American and Scottish notes, in which the starchy formality of Cambridge was contrasted unfavourably with the exuberant warmth of Dublin.

It was my first direct experience of Ireland: Dublin on St Patrick's Eve and St Patrick's Day itself; riding along O'Connell Street in a jaunting car, en route to the final match of the hurling season; laughing, teasing crowds in the street, and at the ground—during the match; keen debating and continuous good talk; the St Patrick's Ball, with Irish music to stir the stiffest feet to nimbleness where I could have danced 'The Walls of Limerick' for days; the lively girl with red hair, green eyes, high cheekbones and delicate fair skin, who might have been the heroine of one of the great tales of ancient Ireland; a student from Northern Ireland, at Trinity College, whose tartan kilt was regarded as an affectation by students from University College; a visit with Sean O'Connor to the relics of the Easter Rising, when we stood together silently and gazed at his Uncle Michael's blood-stained greatcoat; the crowded Mass in the University church in Stephen's Green; the Wicklow Mountains viewed in a rapid afternoon excursion; everywhere hospitality, and more hospitality, as if it would never end; happy tiredness on the boat back to Glasgow's Broomielaw, and a warm affection for the Irish now that I had seen them at home. I had felt entirely at home among them.

Two queries arose after I had settled again in Edinburgh. Ireland, or Dublin at any rate, had appeared to an extraordinary degree classless; or, at least, untroubled by class distinction among the native Irish. There were indeed deep political differences, but they seemed little affected by class, if you discounted the relics of English imperial ascendancy. How long could this last was the first question. The second had to do with religion. The students whom I met were all Christians, mainly Catholic, and showed no doctrinal uneasiness as far as I could see. There was, however, a marked degree of anti-clericalism in student company when parents or clergy were not around. Usually good-humoured, occasionally bitter, it suggested that the younger, educated laity would not submit to clerical domination for long. How long? 'Oh! I think for another thirty or so years!' replied one student, drily; 'it won't be easy to change that!' Disagreement with clergy about politics was familiar to me already, of course, but anti-clericalism as encountered in France and, more mildly, in Ireland, was a new phenomenon. The intensity of some French anti-clerical feeling had made me think again of the Spanish situation, and the wild hatred and anger expressed there in butchery of priests and nuns and destruction of churches. The Church in Spain had suffered from too much privilege through many centuries, and in spite of various revolutions. The Church, in an independent Ireland free at last from English government, would have to face problems created by too privileged an association with the state, too close identification with worldly power and wealth. *The Catholic Worker*, which I had got to know in Whiterigg, proclaimed the Church's primary duty towards the poor. That was not disputed by Christians, at least as theory. But there was surely a duty also to thinkers, those so easily dismissed as 'intellectuals' by fideist, authoritarian clergy who had never dared to admit, to themselves even, that we are obliged by faith to search for understanding and to use our God-given minds to explore the truth which we profess. The students who used the Edinburgh Dominican Chaplaincy library, some of those met in Dublin, and a growing number of professional people in general, looked for a religion which faced intellectual difficulties instead of avoiding them in the hope that they would go away if ignored for long enough.

Archbishop Macdonald was aware of the situation, and worried by the number of people who were drifting away from the Church in Scotland—what was referred to as 'the leakage problem'. He was told that Frank Sheed, the publisher, had a method of teaching religion, wrote to ask what it was, and invited him to Edinburgh to discuss the matter. Sheed has described in his book *The Church and I* how, early in 1939, 600 teachers sat for four afternoons in succession while he exposed the inadequacy of religious education. Teachers, priests and archbishop listened and grew visibly depressed and dismayed.

On the third afternoon two senior university students offered themselves as 'vile bodies' (you remember the old rule—*fiat experimentum in corpore vili*—experiments should be made on cheap material). I treated them both

as a class I was teaching, then gave them the sort of
questions that go with the Evidence Guild teaching
method. They did admirably. Both were converts. Their
performance, I think, lifted everybody's spirits. If so, the
lift did not last. For the final meeting I had asked that a
class of primary school pupils should be brought in who
had received a high mark from the diocesan inspector of
religious teaching. I examined them in the presence of
the Archbishop and the 600. I was not heckling, simply
trying to find out what the catechism answers meant to
them which they gave so accurately, so confidently. It
was very grim.

The two students were Roy Torbet and I. We were conscript
'volunteers'. Roy spoke first, ten minutes on 'Hell'. He was a
sensitive scholar, unused to heckling, and clearly upset by
Sheed's way of jumping aggressively from point to point before
he had finished a reply. My blood boiled. I knew this game.
When my turn came to speak on 'The Four Marks of the
Church', I carried the attack to Sheed.

'Remember what it says in *Habbakuk*, chapter 14!' he retorted
to some statement I had made.

'There you go!' I replied triumphantly: 'I *thought* you didn't
know the Bible! or maybe you have one invented privately! In
any ordinary Bible, the prophecy of Habbakuk has only three
chapters. And that is true in Protestant and Catholic Bibles alike!'
The audience was thrilled by such knockabout stuff. There was
tremendous applause when Sheed cried truce, saying,

'You see it takes a convert; one who knows his Bible!' The
intended follow-up was to be arrested by the outbreak of war in
the autumn, but that day was one that affected my thinking
about what to do after university.

It was relevant to ask why I remained at university. This
question had been put early in the session 1938–39 by the new
professor of British History, Basil Williams' successor, V. H.
Galbraith. Our conversation went something like this.

'We are worried about you, Mr Ross. Do you, or do you not,
want a First?'

'I really don't care, professor, whether I get a degree.'

'Then what are you doing here?'

'I think I am being educated, but mainly outside classrooms.

I came here hoping to be trained as a historian, but that is not being done.'

'Not being done? What is done, then?'

'We are given secondary authorities to read and memorise all the time. We hardly ever deal with sources. There's no palaeography unless one does Scottish history. When we have sources they are usually treated uncritically. Professor Watt was flipping through Ignatius of Antioch the other day, saying it was all perfectly clear: *episcopos* equalled *minister*, *presbuteroi* equalled *elders*, and that was that! He made no attempt to support his interpretation. It was a sheer waste of time. Most of the lecture room work is. We could read the books for ourselves. There's no need to have somebody paraphrasing Tout's *Advanced History* for us!'

'Hm! Are you doing any relevant work at present?'

'Something in church history. And I'm attempting the kind of thing I had hoped to be taught, editing a selection from a sixteenth-century Scottish text, *The Gude and Godlie Ballatis*. It's going to be published.'

'I see. Well! Perhaps I should not say this, but I agree with your views. I hope that I may change things, but it will take five or six years, too long for you. In the meantime I will not worry about you and you need not worry about me.'

'Thank you, professor!' I said, with an astonishing feeling of relief, and turned to go.

'By the way,' he added, 'do you intend to sit Finals?'

'Yes,' I answered, 'to please my family, and the people at the Catholic chaplaincy, who expect it.'

He nodded, and the interview was over. One decision had been made at least. I ought to have taken final examinations in May of 1938, but had not fulfilled all the conditions. Now I was committed to May, 1939, and would have to tackle one more subject outside the History Group; philosophy or political economy, neither of much interest to me at that particular point in time, when a brain-child was a fair way to being born, in the shape of a series of *Scottish Classics*.

Experience, especially in the Scottish Literature Society, had shown the difficulty of extending knowledge of Scottish writers when little work was available in print. A vicious circle existed between readers and texts; a chicken and egg puzzle which could be resolved perhaps if cheap texts were provided for students and prescribed by professors for study in literature classes. Selections would be better than complete texts, for obvious reasons. As a start I thought four volumes might appear simultaneously; selections from the *Gude and Godlie Ballatis*; John Knox's *History of the Reformation in Scotland*; poems of Allan Ramsay; and of James Hogg. Dr John Oliver, then lecturing in literature at Moray House College of Education, considered the scheme good and suggested an approach to Oliver and Boyd, the publishers. Their managing director, Ainslie Thin, liked the idea. Could I assemble a sufficiently impressive editorial committee? Had I thought of approaching the Saltire Society, which would undoubtedly take a practical interest in such a venture? He thought slim hardback volumes preferable to the paperback brochures suggested in my outline plan. The Saltire Society liked the idea and it was proposed that the projected series should be known as *The Saltire Scottish Classics*. The Society, founded as recently as 1936 was enjoying a first flush of energy and its support was immensely valuable. An editorial committee was set up without difficulty, consisting of Sir Herbert Grierson, Sir John Oliver, Mr Harvey Wood and myself. The other members had to be persuaded that the volume of selections from the *Gude and Godlie Ballatis* was a sound idea, because in fact they were not very familiar with the book. One meeting however was enough to reach agreement that four volumes should be launched in the Spring of 1940. They were: *The Gude and Godlie Ballatis*, edited by Ian Ross, *John Knox's Historie of the Reformation in Scotland*, edited by Ralph S. Walker, *Selected Poems*, by James Hogg, edited by J. W. Oliver, and *Selected Poems*, by Allan Ramsay, edited by H. Harvey Wood. Each was priced at 3/6 with postage 3d extra. Two more volumes were to be published later: *Scott's Songs*, edited by Sir Herbert Grierson and *Selections from Urquhart*, edited by John Purves.

23

Acceptance of the Scottish Classics project, by the Saltire Society and Messrs Oliver & Boyd, prompted a decision at last about what to aim at after university: a career in publishing. Publishing could be creative, a contribution towards development of a better society, a means of serving God and man together. And hour with Frank Sheed, of Sheed & Ward, settled the matter. He offered a six months trial in London with his firm, to begin about the end of September, 1939. If found satisfactory, I would become eventually manager of the British section of the firm. The starting salary of four pounds a week appeared sufficient. A load lifted from my mind. There was relief at home; Dad was pleased.

Some friends were surprised, thinking that I should become a priest. Since early childhood there had been people who destined me to wear a clerical collar, as Presbyterian minister or Catholic priest. Their certainty was always greater than mine. For one thing, celibacy seemed too difficult a commitment for me, and that ruled out serious thought of priesthood. In any case the question could not arise for several years, because I was heavily in debt, and life in London on four pounds weekly would not allow much saving towards repayment. I would coast along gently to Finals, enjoy a relaxed summer—and then to London! That was the prospect in the autumn of 1938, and it looked good, until one afternoon in Edinburgh when I went to tea with John Barry and his wife Dorothy.

Mrs Barry asked how everything was at home. 'Very good indeed!' was the answer. The next question:

'Is your father more reconciled to your being a Catholic?' I laughed:

'Amazingly! I don't think he would object even if I became a priest.' There was silence.

'Why don't you?' said Mrs Barry. The reply to that was simple:

'Oh, there are several solid reasons for not even considering the idea.' John Barry looked at his wife, then,

'Would you mind my asking if one of the reasons is financial?'

'Not at all! It's well known that I'm in debt, quite heavily.' They looked at each other; it was not hard to suspect what was coming.

'If the question is not too personal,' he said, 'would you mind telling us how much you owe?'

'Ninety pounds.' He replied at once:

'If that is what stands between you and priesthood we would be happy to remove the obstacle.'

I sat stunned.

'Would it be black or white?' asked Mrs Barry, meaning by that, would I apply for admission to the diocesan priesthood or to the Dominican Order.

'I don't know. I haven't really thought about it. I need to think.'

'There is no hurry,' John Barry remarked, 'but in any case we would like to clear the debts now.' I managed to make some kind of grateful acknowledgment of their offer and got away as soon as was decently possible, confused and scared by such a direct challenge.

I discussed it with Kitty Macleod, who was Presbyterian. She thought I could 'do more good as a priest than in any other way.' At the chaplaincy the suggestion that I might apply for admission to the Dominican Order was received with daunting coolness by Father Fabian, and by Father Giles. Said the latter, 'You would have to see the Provincial, if you did decide to apply. He probably won't want to take you, because he's sure there's going to be a war.' It became clear that Father Giles thought that my being a conscientious objector would make acceptance unlikely.

But why think only of the Dominican Order? There were others, for example the Franciscans. Medieval history had made Francis of Assisi familiar, a well-loved figure whose emphasis on poverty was wholly in keeping with the Gospel. But modern Franciscans were different and, I suppose, they were little in favour of study. To become a Benedictine monk it would be necessary—again I supposed—to sing fairly well, which ruled me out. My room-mate, a good Episcopalian, imagined me as a Jesuit, in which he was not alone. Among Jesuits there was the attractive, inspiring figure of Father Martindale, author of *What are Saints?* and much else. Was he typical of the grim Society? Like many other people at the time, I supposed not. In any case

blind, military obedience was what Jesuits had to undertake, I
imagined; and such obedience appeared impossible to combine
with obedience to Christ. Dominicans, the Order of Preachers,
as illustrated by the three men at the Edinburgh chaplaincy,
were individual and human, combining prayer and study,
humorous and intelligent, and visibly managing to live together
in charity, although so different from each other in background
and personality; and I knew them at first hand. But what about
the diocesan priesthood, the everyday ministry on which the
Church depended? Was it not preferable?

Discussion, during the next vacation, with Canon Grant in
Beauly and with my father, was helpful. Between two Sundays
the Canon was in communication with the Bishop of Aberdeen.
There would be a place for me next autumn in the Scots College
in Rome, the Bishop said, if I wished to be considered for the
diocese. I was very doubtful, although the prospect of study in
Rome was exciting. Priests in the Aberdeen diocese, with its huge
scattered parishes, were often very isolated. It was said of one
parish that any man sent there for more than a very few years
became a contemplative or an alcoholic; the latter would be more
likely in my case, I told the Canon. He laughed ruefully. He
had asked someone else who was proposing to join an Order,
'Can't you save your soul in your own diocese?' only to be told
firmly 'I don't think so!'

My father asked many questions about the Dominicans and
their work. He appreciated the value of living in community,
and the importance of celibacy. Community living was not
strange to Highland people, and there were many among us who
never married because of strong commitment to family or
profession. What did seem strange to Dad was the idea of not
possessing any personal property. 'Would it not be better,' he
asked, 'to become a priest like the Canon, with your own house
and money? He's a holy man, although he has both.' A long
discussion ended with his saying: 'Well, it's your own life, and
you must do with it what you think best. Anyway, if you have
holidays, you will be welcome here always.' That was an
encouraging statement with which to go back to Edinburgh;
there would be no bitterness at home, at least on my father's
part, if I did enter the noviciate. There was my grandmother to
be considered, but it seemed better not to risk upsetting her,
when no decision had been reached—and in Edinburgh it looked

very uncertain that the Order would accept me as a novice, no matter what my wish might be.

The Prior Provincial, Father Bernard Delany, head of the Order in Great Britain, interviewed me in the course of a routine visit to Edinburgh. He was a gentle man, with a melancholy bloodhound face, and a vague manner which fitted his reputation for indecision. Plainly he was worried by pacifism and talked about 'just war' for a few minutes, before dropping the subject with a disarmingly apologetic smile and the remark that he was no specialist in such matters. Looking out of the window and twiddling a window cord, he expressed his conviction that there would be war in the very near future. 'There probably won't be a noviciate, until it is all over', he added lugubriously. The interview ended with an assurance that in due course, if I sent in the appropriate form, he would let me know what was decided about my application. That conversation took place somewhere about April, certainly at least several weeks before the start of final examinations; but week followed week without any letter from Father Bernard. The international outlook grew worse. I decided that after the results of Finals were published, and whatever might happen in the meantime, I should go home and tell my grandmother that I intended to study for priesthood.

In due course the list of passes in history appeared in *The Scotsman*, with my name among those who were awarded second-class honours. That was enough for home and school. I lacked a degree pass in one necessary subject outside the history honours group, but lacked money and inclination to do any more towards graduating. Much had been given me in the university but, beyond doubt, the time to leave it had come. It was high time also to go home and tell Granny what my intentions were. And what was to be done about Sheed & Ward, as weeks stretched into months, with no communication from the Dominican Prior Provincial? Home first, was the decision; next, write urgently to the Provincial; then to Mr Sheed, hopefully after having received some reply from Father Delany.

Home. The 'Old Lady', my grandmother, was sitting on a low chair. The Gaelic New Testament was lying on her lap, open at St John's Gospel. I knelt beside her. She listened closely as I spoke of necessity of trying to commit myself totally to the following of Christ, and of where the way of doing so might lie for me. She took my hands in hers, tears falling quietly over her face as she listened. When I finished:

'We will never see each other again,' she said. She was eighty years of age. I was in tears also as I answered,

'Not in this life but, please God, in the next.' She made no protest. That night I read to her as usual, but went away early next morning with her blessing. We had never, at any time, quarrelled about religion.

In Edinburgh uncertainty was the name of the situation. The League of Nations had failed to stop Mussolini's African outrage. Hitler had been getting his own way increasingly, and those who believed that he meant what he wrote in *Mein Kampf* were deeply depressed. Koestler's *Darkness at Noon* reflected what was happening in Russia. Socialism had destroyed itself in Spain by its own disunity, more deadly than foreign intervention in support of Franco. To be a pacifist in such a world was to commit oneself to failure; the alternative was also failure, disastrous failure for the human race. There could be no hope in politics until moral principles mattered not only to a few ineffectual idealists, but to the bulk of the electorate and those whom they selected to exercise power on their behalf. The most that a pacifist minority in Britain could hope to achieve was to secure decent treatment for conscientious objectors and, if war came, to moderate hatred and hysteria, and help to keep alive ideas of a just settlement after the fighting.

When war did come, in September 1939, there was no excitement, no patriotic singing, only a widespread hope that it would be over soon. Most members of the Student Pacifist Association had decided to accept whatever forms of non-combatant service might be offered to them by tribunals. Three of us went one evening in September to a meeting of conscientious objectors and immediately after it met three of our friends walking up Chambers Street. They had volunteered that afternoon for military service, with no desire to be involved in war but judging it better not to wait for conscription. They were reluctant soldiers, bowing to inevitability because, they said, they had no strong will for any other action. 'We're not likely to meet again,' said one, 'what about going for a drink?' It was agreed, gloomily. We began in Drummond Street, then down to Hunter Square, along Rose Street pub by pub and up into Lothian Road, where we decided to find food in a licensed restaurant which is no longer there. After one of the party had been sick in a washbasin we were asked to leave, and shook the

dust of the place from our feet with drunken solemnity. I made
some scathing remarks to the doorman before clambering after
the others into a taxi, which delivered us to the respectable street
near Churchhill in which the youngest of the group then lodged.
His formidable landlady was a friend of his mother and it was
important that he should reach his room undetected. A student
called Mair, and I, were comparatively sober; leaving the others
on the pavement we saw our friend climb the stairs successfully,
on hands and knees, before closing the front door behind us
very gently. Two others were persuaded to rise from the
pavement, and then consented to be taken home without further
difficulty. The fourth, unaccustomed to heavy drinking, was in
a sorry state. We had to undress and bath him, before getting
him into bed. Nobody stirred in the house as we worked swiftly
and silently at our necessary task, before slipping out into the
Meadows, where we sat on a bench for a while and reviewed the
evening. At about two-thirty in the morning we parted.

Six hours later Miss Clemmy came into my room, to say that
Father Fabian had arrived with an urgent message. He came in
behind her with a telegram in his hand. In desperation I had
sent a reply-paid telegram to the Provincial: 'Noviciate. Yes or
no?' The reply read: 'Retreat begins 3 p.m. Woodchester 14
September.' That was all. The 14th was the following day.
Woodchester Priory, then the English Dominican noviciate
house, was nine miles or more beyond Gloucester, and I had
nothing ready. As Father Fabian remarked drily, there was much
to do before catching the night train from Edinburgh which
would allow me to reach Woodchester in time for the retreat.

My room-mate, Bill McKinnell, offered to get my books
across to the chaplaincy, where they would remain in an attic
until the future was clearer. Any papers could go there also, in a
small trunk. Clothes were no problem, as I had very few. As
someone had noted at coffee one morning, 'If your clothes are
OK, your shoes are in bits, and vice-versa!' Now, however,
clothes of a particular kind were required—white shirts, long
white stockings, a dark suit, and a black soft hat—which meant
that part of the day had to be spent shopping, largely at the
chaplaincy's expense, as I did not have enough money for clothes
and for the train journey that night. The clothes prescription
came as a surprise, because the Dominicans in Edinburgh did
not seem very fussy about their own clothes and were certainly

not restricted to white shirts, as every washing day made evident. It was a tiring day, shopping with a hangover from the night before. The brightest moment was when Father Aelred was told what was happening. He had heard nothing about my attempts to become a novice, and his spontaneous delight at the news was immensely heart-warming. Here was one Dominican at least with enthusiasm for the idea!

The train was due to leave Edinburgh somewhere about ten or eleven, and Father Fabian came to see me off. 'I think you may need this on the journey,' he remarked, handing over a half bottle of brandy. The train was crammed with people, as trains would be normally throughout the war. Blackout everywhere; unexplained halts. We were eight in our dim compartment, I in a corner seat opposite a talkative young sailor who had a bottle of whisky still three-quarters full. He offered it round the compartment but it was refused amiably by everyone, except me. He accepted the brandy bottle, but after a cautious taste shook his head and went back to whisky. The woman on my left fell asleep, and her head fell on my shoulder, inhibiting movement, as I did not like to disturb her sleep. A fitful doze; stiff neck; alcoholic weariness; the sailor snored; the train stopped, jerked forward, stopped again, for no obvious reason; a slow, awkward passage to and from the toilet, tripping and disturbing the other passengers in the compartment and the wedged bodies in the corridor; unidentifiable stations; the train crawled and the stops in the darkness grew increasingly frustrating. We came to Gloucester at last, crumby and unwashed. Eventually I found the small local train which would stop at Woodchester, on the branch line which ran in those days from Gloucester to Nailsworth.

I walked slowly up a steep hill to the Priory of the Annunciation, a range of convincingly weathered Victorian Gothic architecture, in time for lunch; met five assorted characters who were also prospective novices; handed over to the novice-master the half-empty bottle of brandy and seventeen shillings, which was all the money I had left. The day dragged on somehow. What I wanted most of all was sleep. Ten o'clock, and 'lights out', came none too soon.

24

Woodchester Priory was associated with an Oxford Movement convert to Roman obedience, William Leigh, a wealthy Yorkshire manufacturer, who built the church in 1848 for the Passionist Mission led by the Venerable Dominic Barberi. The Passionists soon decided that Woodchester was too remote from industrial England to serve their purpose, and Leigh offered the church and some adjoining property to the Dominicans who, at that point, were considering emigrating to North America as only half a dozen of them survived in Britain, where they seemed to have no future. William Leigh's offer of Woodchester was welcomed as a providential assurance of new life. After 1850 there were novices and the Order, which Newman had described as a great ideal unfortunately extinct, was coming to life again in England, as it had done already in France with Henri Lacordaire and his companions.

'New Life' is perhaps not the most exact description of what was developing around 1850; 'restoration' might be a more appropriate term. There was a vigorous attempt to restore the past, as reconstructed by romantic imagination. This was reflected in life-style and in architecture. Under the reforming French Master of the Order, Jandel, 'primitive observance' was the ideal, a fiercely ascetic pattern of living to be achieved in appropriately medieval style buildings. The priory at Woodchester formed a quadrangle on the hillside four miles south of Stroud, opposite Amberley, with a large fruit and vegetable garden above it, and brewery and bakery in the crypt. There were chickens to produce eggs. Total abstinence from meat was the rule at Woodchester in the nineteenth century and the community aimed at a large degree of independence in food production.

The cells of the brethren were small, and furnished very simply. Each had a narrow iron bedstead, a small wooden table with a matching chair, a wooden *prie-dieu*, and a shelf in an angle of the room, to hold a washbasin and ewer. There was also a small chest of drawers, and a hook or two on the back of the door; so there was ample provision for keeping one's clothes.

Above the washbasin there was a small mirror; above the *prie-dieu* a crucifix. The wooden floor was bare. The walls were painted or distempered white, or pale yellow. Nothing had changed much between 1850 and 1939, except that in a large section of the building the iron pipe which ran through each cell was cold, because the central heating plant was partly out of order. So it was to remain through the very severe winter of 1939–40, when water often froze overnight in our ewers.

There were three categories of person in the community; priests, laybrothers, and novices, each with its own common room for purposes of recreation and communication, The prior, the bursar, and the novice-master had each two cells; one personal, the other serving as an office in which they saw members of the community when necessary. Otherwise brethren were forbidden to enter each other's cells. When communication was necessary, it took place briefly at a cell door or, if unavoidably lengthy, in the appropriate common room. By rule the categories did not mix, and silence was the rule in the cloister; but on Christmas Day, Easter Sunday, and at some other great feasts, everyone met in the priests' common room for one or more hours of recreation. Ordinarily all the brethren ate together in the refectory, in total silence at breakfast but to an accompaniment of reading aloud at other meals. Seating was in order of seniority, within the categories, but with the prior, sub-prior, and novice-master at the head of the refectory. In addition to the church and the refectory there was one other place where everyone assembled regularly, namely the chapter room. There was supposed to be a 'chapter of faults' once a week, with everyone seated in order of seniority on the bench which ran round the room, the prior presiding at the apex of the assembly. He delivered a homily, and then drew attention to points of observance which the brethren should consider more carefully, or to details of domestic economy and management. After that, one by one, the members of the community stood up and stepped forward, beginning with the youngest, to accuse themselves of such faults as breaking silence in the cloister without good reason, or neglecting cleaning duties, or speaking to strangers. It could be funny at times. 'I accuse myself of being late for Mass, and of being careless when serving in the refectory, and spilling soup over two of the brothers.' But for novices it was a hard trial at times. By ancient custom, brethren

were expected also to accuse each other, but by 1939 English
principles had asserted themselves to suppress that practice.
After the general house chapter, lay brothers, and novices, had
their separate chapters.

The usual time for rising was 5.25. One of the brethren went
round, knocked on each door, threw it open, and called
Benedicamus Domino (let us bless the Lord) to which the
expected reply was *Deo Gratias*! (thanks to God!). Prayers began
in church at 5.45, the community in two facing banks of seats,
in the choir. Half an hour was spent in silent meditation,
followed by the Community Mass which was sung more often
than not. Mass and prayers—'the Divine Office'—were of course
in Latin, and the music was Gregorian chant. Prayers consisted,
for the most part, of the Psalms of David, recited in a monotone
except on Sundays and some major festivals, when Lauds or
Vespers might be sung, again in plain chant.

Breakfast was about 7.45 or 8 o'clock—brown bread and
butter with bowls of coffee. From 14 September, (the Feast of
the Exaltation of the Cross) until Easter Sunday, was fasting
time, the 'Long Fast', during which four ounces was the
maximum amount of bread allowed for breakfast. The main meal
of the day was at 12.15, following about fifteen minutes of
prayer. It consisted nearly always of three courses: soup, main
course, pudding. Meat was allowed at three meals each week, by
dispensation from headquarters in Rome, given out of
consideration for the 'Teutonic stomach' and the northern
climate. Fish on Wednesdays and Fridays added further variety
to what was predominantly a vegetarian diet. At 6 p.m. there was
a second half-hour of meditation in church, followed by
recitation of the Rosary and Compline; then came supper, eight
to ten ounces of solid food during fasting time, and never meat.
Midday meal and supper were followed by recreation for half an
hour. At nine in the evening, Matins and Lauds were recited,
taking about forty-five minutes, after which Solemn Silence
began, not to be broken until after Mass next morning. In
principle, only something urgent could justify talking during
Solemn Silence.

Such was the overall pattern in the priory. Most of the priests
were engaged in pastoral work in the parish and its nine
dependent outlying Mass centres, which covered between them a
few hundred square miles of Gloucestershire. Some younger

priests were at Woodchester to round off their study of pastoral theology. An older priest, Father Ferdinand Valentine, was employed chiefly in preaching retreats up and down England; he was in the priory only for short intervals between preaching engagements. The lay brothers maintained the domestic routine of the house; one, as sacristan, cared for the church and its furnishing, and the provision of whatever was required for services; another was in charge of the kitchen, another the refectory, a fourth the laundry. The brothers laid tables, washed up after meals, swept and polished corridors, guest rooms and community rooms, everywhere except in the noviciate. Priests were responsible for their own cells.

Priests and brothers together numbered fourteen or fifteen Dominicans who had taken solemn vows. There was a full-time lay employee with a young assistant, to look after the garden and the extensive greenhouses, whose tomato crop made an important contribution towards the gardeners' wages. To some extent, everyone helped in the garden, especially when apples, pears and plums were ready for picking. (Novices helped to pick everything, except strawberries!) A major non-resident contributor to the Community's life was Ozzie Workman, a widower officially retired from work, but never idle, omniscient in regard to drains, poultry, badgers, weeds, repairs, local customs, and the eccentricities of earlier brethren. He was a weathered man with a twinkling eye, which suited his unfailing quiet humour. Slow to comment, Ozzie missed nothing within eye range and remembered it all, but his hearing was less acute than his vision. He had a sort of workshop in what had once been stables, and any excuse to visit him there was welcome. There was warmth in his company, although no fire in his workshop.

Visits to Ozzie were not allowed easily. Novices lived in a small tight community within the priory, locked in their own wing for most of the time, leaving in procession two by two for services in the church and reciting a penitential psalm as they processed along the cloister. No one ever left the noviciate for any reason without a companion. Twice a week there was an afternoon walk, all setting out and returning together although the distance between the fast and the slow widened temporarily on the walk. On Saturday afternoons, after thorough cleaning of the noviciate premises, duly inspected by the novice-master, there was a run in Woodchester Park. Those who enjoyed running ran; those who did not jogged about two hundred yards through the Park gates and then, safe from observation, slowed to a walk.

One hot bath a week was allowed, on Saturday after the run. There were only two baths in the noviciate, so leisurely bathing was out of the question. There was no restriction on cold baths, but our year was not given to such excessive mortification. There was no bathing after the outdoor manual work on Tuesday, Wednesday, and Friday afternoons. Nor was there tea in the afternoon, however cold or wet the weather, until compassionate laybrothers offered to hide a large enamel teapot, cups, milk, and sugar, in the cellar where we changed from our working boots.

Each day was regulated by a timetable designed to leave us scant space alone or unoccupied. In addition to the Divine Office, which we shared with the main community (except the lay brothers, who came only to Mass and Compline) novices recited the 'Little Office' of Our Lady in the noviciate chapel. Every morning at nine o'clock there was spiritual reading in common for half an hour. We took it in turn to read, for about five minutes, from a small manuscript *Rule for Novices* which reminded us that food and drink were not suitable matter for the conversation of religious, that we should not hold hands or have 'particular friendships', and much else that escapes my memory. From time to time passages occasioned fits of giggling, which were liable to happen in church also, during Office. Giggling was infectious, and could involve young priests as well as novices, the older priests then continuing the psalms, sometimes with a smile, sometimes as though nothing untoward was happening.

After listening to the *Rule for Novices*, we remained sitting round our common room table, each reading silently some book which the novice-master had approved. We were not allowed into the Priory's extensive library but had access to between two or three hundred volumes, ancient for the most part, shelved in the noviciate common room. There was enough there to keep my attention, works by Dominican writers and by medieval English mystics. So I read Catherine of Siena, Henry Suso, Tauler, in selection, Humbert of Romans, Vincent Ferrer, Reginald Buckler, Bertrand Wilberforce, Bede Jarrett, Vincent McNabb, even some Thomas Aquinas. There were also numerous biographies which were permitted as 'spiritual reading'. Being a rapid reader, I was able to get through most of them during the noviciate year. Various lives of St Dominic and other Dominican saints, but especially Catherine of Siena, increased my knowledge of Dominican traditions. There were other figures hitherto totally unknown to me, or known very slightly; such as Bartholomew of the Martyrs, Archbishop of Braga, who carried out Tridentine reform in Portugal; Las Casas, who had defended the rights of American Indians in the nascent Spanish empire; Mother Margaret Hallahan, working to exhaustion among the poor of nineteenth century industrial England; fourteenth century travellers in the East, Savonarola, Lacordaire, martyrs in Japan, Indo-China, Europe. The Dominican garden was, as Catherine of Siena had remarked, very varied.

Our reading was not confined to Dominican material. Jesuits were well represented by St Ignatius Loyola himself, by Père Grou, de Caussade, Lallemant, Goodier, Martindale, and the historical work of Father Broderick. De Caussade's *Treatise on Abandonment to Divine Providence* was a major discovery in my life, read and read again, very slowly. Notebooks which have survived show that other books which made a deep impression were Wallis Budge's *Paradise of the Fathers*, St Catherine's *Dialogue*, Julian of Norwich's *Revelations of Divine Love*, Henry Suso's *Little Book of Eternal Wisdom*, the anonymous *Cloud of Unknowing*, Buckler's *Perfection of Man by Charity*, and St Augustine's sermons on the psalms and on St John, read in the old Oxford translation, the volumes of which were brought by the novice-master from the priory library.

A small part of the bookshelves was occupied by a selection of English literature intended for recreational reading and, it may be presumed, for the fuller education of those who became novices at sixteen or seventeen. One of my contemporaries was a lively seventeen-year-old extrovert, to whom the collected works of Dickens, Scott, Jane Austen, Thackeray, Trollope, Stevenson, Shakespeare, Tennyson, and Pope were blissfully unknown, saving such burdens in a schoolboy's life as *Ivanhoe*, *David Copperfield*, *Julius Caesar* and *Treasure Island*. Thackeray I had dismissed as a bore, after venturing prematurely on *Pendennis* at the age of thirteen. Trollope, however, was completely new, and I wandered happily in Barset and its environs for an hour every Sunday evening throughout the year at Woodchester.

Our only newspapers were *The Times*, brought up a day late from the priests' common room, and two religious weekly papers, the *Catholic Herald* and the *Universe*. We had no radio. Television of course was still a dream, but would have been banned, like wireless, had it been invented. Our world was heavily restricted. On our afternoon walks as at other times it was forbidden to speak to 'seculars'. Having no money we could not patronise shops or pubs, which was one of the reasons why we walked in the country, mile after mile, avoiding towns or large villages, in which we would have been like the Bisto Twins, gazing forlornly through privileged windows.

Every morning after spiritual reading there were classes in Christian doctrine, the Order's constitutions, liturgy, and plain chant. These were all conducted by the novice-master. In the first few months there was also reading practice in the refectory. There was a morning interval, from ten-thirty to eleven o'clock, when we walked silently in the garden. There were compulsory periods of recreation, in the noviciate common room, after lunch and after supper. Between four-thirty and six o'clock, and again from about eight to nine o'clock, we were alone in our cells; the latter period was 'free' reading time, which distinguished it from the 'private spiritual reading' for which the earlier period was intended. Lights went out in the noviciate at ten o'clock, every night, and none too early in view of the rising hour. Getting up was hard, especially for the man who was caller of the week. He might feel so burdened by responsibility that his sleep was broken, and that involved a danger of falling into very deep sleep between four and five in the morning, and failing to do the caller's round in time. There was one occasion when an anxious novice leaped from bed and dashed round, exclaiming at each door, '*Benedicamus Domino*! I'm sorry I'm late!' until an irritated novice-master stopped him with the words, 'Get back to bed, brother! It is only two o'clock!' It was some small comfort to be told by the assistant novice-master that after thirty years in the Order he still found it difficult to rise on time; but everyone knew that he spent ages in church every night when most of us were sleeping.

We novices were a curious bunch, ranging in age from 17 to 36, with differences in social and educational background to match variation in age. One was already a sub-deacon, from a seminary in France, and would leave after six months, to the relief of the rest of us, who found his humourless and rigid view of life very hard to live with amicably. (After the Second Vatican Council he became notable briefly as one of the few English priests who aligned themselves with Archbishop Lefebvre.) Another, with a famous public school and Oxford behind him, suffered from severe constipation with immense good humour for eight months, finding relief at last on the day following his decision to leave the noviciate. A third, from South Africa, was a librarian by profession. He was openly disdainful of our two teenagers, especially the younger whose exuberance and uncritical enthusiasm for everything Dominican strained his patience and understanding. He suffered throughout the winter from the severe cold, and the sparse near-vegetarian diet, his chilblains little helped by woollen mittens. Winter he had expected. The English summer was too much to endure. After two months of that he returned to South Africa, became a lay Dominican, was ordained eventually to the priesthood in a South African diocese, and died a few years after ordination.

The three youngest of us remained to survive the noviciate year, and more; our given 'religious' names Lucian, Adrian and Anthony. Although senior in years I was youngest in precedence, my clothing as a novice having been delayed for some uncomfortable weeks as the Provincial had failed to process my application fully. As a convert I had to have a dispensation from Rome to allow me to be received as a novice,—and he had delayed applying for it, or it was held up in the post. Pending its arrival I made a ten day retreat with everyone else, but remained half-dressed in a tunic and belt while the other beginners went around in full Dominican habit of tunic, scapular, capuce and rosary. Worst of all was the fact that their heads were shaven, whereas the bushy long hair with which I had arrived at Woodchester grew longer and wilder. 'The sooner you go the better!' growled one of the priests as we passed one morning in the cloister.

Still more depressing was a session with the Prior, who had been instructed by the Provincial to educate me in the theology of war. The Prior was a pleasant character who had never lived, as boy or man, outside the shelter of the Order, with which his family had long and close association. He had studied Scripture at the École Biblique in Jerusalem for a time, was granted a Master's degree in theology at an early age, and it was doubtful if he had studied very much after that. His talents were atrophied by the dogmatic assurance which marked the particular neo-scholastic position adopted by most teachers in the Order, and in the English Province, at that time. When I entered his room, uncertain as to why the novice-master had sent me there, he took down from its shelf a volume of St Thomas Aquinas's *Summa Theologica* and read, in English, part of what Thomas wrote about the possibility of waging a just war. Closing the volume, he smiled and said brightly:

'Well, there it is!' There was an increasingly uncomfortable silence in which we regarded each other, each waiting. At last I replied,

'I've read St Thomas, but isn't there more to it than that?'

'What, for example?' he asked, with a lift of eyebrows with which I was to become very familiar.

'Other Dominicans, for one thing. Someone like Vittoria, or even now Father Gerald Vann, whose articles I've read. Surely thinking has developed since Aquinas?'

'Father Gerald Vann? Very few people agree with his views!' He put Aquinas back on the shelf and remarked in kindly tones,

'You are young yet. You will know better when you are older!'

The interview ended, but a few days later there was a letter from the Provincial which stated sharply that novices came to learn, not to try to teach their superiors.

The Prior seemed determined to stress that idea in various contexts. One day two of us were digging a piece of ground which had been idle for many years, and as we went along we removed carefully any roots of dock, dandelion or nettle; and there were many! The Prior came along and declared that we were too slow. 'There's no need to take out those roots! Just dig them in,' he added. 'But then they will grow again,' I ventured to say. 'Nonsense! Get on with it.' We got on with it, and a great growth of weeds resulted. Even more annoying was his behaviour when Peter Anson's book *The Catholic Church in Scotland* was being read at lunchtime. On various occasions he insisted that readers, including me, should adopt his mispronunciation of Scottish names. At least he did not attempt to make me substitute 'lock' for 'loch'.

Such experiences underlined two problems conveniently labelled 'Obedience' and 'Truth'. Dominicans take one explicit vow, a vow of obedience. The motto of the Order is '*Veritas*'— in English 'Truth'. During the retreat which we made in September, the preacher, Father John Baptist Reeves, OP, said much about both subjects, sometimes to the accompaniment of tears, for which he was noted among the brethren. When I had gone to see him in his room and expressed anxiety about obedience, he had looked at me earnestly and remarked, 'That is a great grace, for which to thank God.' What else he said is forgotten; at any rate it did not remove the problem of what sort of obedience we were to consider undertaking. A Prior who is obstinately ignorant about the nature of nettles and dandelions, and the correct pronunciation of the name MacDonald, might be shrugged aside. He was ignorant, but there was no need to make an issue of that fact, but his attitude did raise a question of principle none the less. Was obedience meant to be total, unquestioning, acceptance of commands? Where did personal responsibility fit in? Could one surrender conscience to someone else's control, without reservation? When one knew certainly that those in authority were mistaken, how could this authority be accepted seriously? But how could anyone be sure what was true, or what was just, or who was in error?

We argued about such points, during afternoon walks and sometimes during evening recreation. Some held the view that there was no point in keeping what they considered silly rules of behaviour, such as the rule about not talking unnecessarily during manual work, or one about when our hoods should be worn up, over our heads, and when they should be down on our shoulders. I could see no reason for *not* observing such rules. The brethren were more sensible than members of some orders, were reputed to be; at least *we* were most unlikely ever to be told to scrub a floor with a toothbrush. But had such an order been given I would have obeyed it, just as I obeyed the order to dig in weeds, because it did not conflict with directives from higher authority expressed in the Order's constitution, or in the Church's laws, or in the gospel of Jesus Christ. It seemed to me that the very fact that there was a hierarchy of authority demanded a consciousness of each level of teaching, which would set up problems inevitably if lower authority conflicted with higher authority. 'It's not law that matters, but love!' Colin said

furiously one afternoon. I agreed, but added that law seemed
necessary to correct tendencies which conflicted with true love.
'But if you love you don't need law! Love and do what you will,
St Augustine says,' he retorted. 'But when I don't know if I
love, or how to love, isn't law necessary? To keep one on the
right path?' 'Oh, yes!' he replied, 'maybe in great matters. But
what's the point in taking petty regulations seriously? You don't
do it yourself, drinking tea in the crypt!' He had a point there;
my breach of the rule about tea was inconsistent with the point
I was making, and it was no defence to say that I took tea only
when very cold or wet. Being more used to rough weather, and
being perhaps thicker-skinned, I could do without tea more
easily than my shivering, chilblain-afflicted brethren. By
refusing tea one felt some association with thousands of refugees
deprived not simply of comfort, but of necessary things by war.
But, was refusal of tea not a reflection on those who took it?
Was it not at least implicitly judgmental? Afraid of being accused
of showing a self-righteous attitude towards others, I began to
take tea regularly, and enjoyed it, although always with some
pricking of conscience.

A passage in Paul's letter to the Philippians seemed to take us
to the root of the matter, to my way of thinking.

> Have this mind among yourselves, which was in Christ
> Jesus, who, though he was in the form of God, did not
> count equality with God a thing to be grasped, but
> emptied himself, taking the form of a servant, being born
> in the likeness of men. And being found in human form
> he humbled himself and became obedient unto death,
> even death on a cross.
> (*Philippians* Chapter 2. v–vii).

We were to empty ourselves, through obedience, as Christ did.
Through obedience we might learn 'to die unto self,' to
subordinate our own interests in the interests of others.
Obedience should be an antidote to selfishness and conceit. 'All
very well!' said Vivian, 'but can't it be also an escape from moral
responsibility? Can't it foster self-righteousness and spiritual
pride?' Admittedly he had a point. Given the difficulty of sorting
out tangled motives for action, these could be a real temptation
to abdicate responsibility. 'All authority comes from God' was a
commonplace principle in religious circles. 'If I do what I am

told by lawful authority I can be sure that I am doing the will of God' was the guiding thought for many members of the Church, especially those in religious Orders.

This principle was applied not only in religion, but in politics, sanctioned, it was thought, by Scripture. The Prior had asked me if I considered that I knew better than the government whether a war was just or not. I had tried to explain why, in the light of history and of knowledge of contemporary events, it appeared unreasonable simply to trust governments. The novice-master could appreciate that conscientious objection to military service might arise from someone's personal understanding of a call to follow Christ. The Prior was unable to accept even that; he seemed to believe sincerely that British governments, at least, were to be trusted completely. They would not lie under any circumstances, although they might find it prudent to withhold information occasionally from the public. In his view, if our government decided on war, with at least tacit support from the bishops, there should be no moral problem for the individual Christian. I had remarked that the record suggested that hierarchies fall in predictably behind national governments. The overwhelming majority of bishops in England had followed Henry VIII into schism, an impressive example of what the collective wisdom of a national hierarchy might do.

Vivian and David were in agreement with me, regarding the political issue. Where we differed was about the significance of the day-to-day directives in community life; the rubrics which governed the Divine Office, the community's timetable, the rules about food, and silence, the library, the garden, recreation, dress. These rules, so often tiresome, were a means of self-emptying in my view; there was no moral necessity to question them and our discussion became a wasteful expenditure of time and energy, the more it was continued. The issues were from one point of view very simple; my natural indolence and self-indulgence were challenged by the monastic timetable, my aggressiveness and love of fighting were challenged by Christ directly, however condoned by church or state. And so I gave careful attention to rubrics and details of the Order's constitutions, while refusing to change my position about war. The Provincial wrote to say that he respected my position although unable to agree with it, but that in the event of a summons to appear before the tribunal for conscientious objectors I would have to leave Woodchester and the noviciate. After the war, he added, it would be possible to begin again. In the event I was not summoned, being covered by the terms of exemption from military service, for theology students, agreed soon afterwards by the church and the government.

Correspondence with my father became more painful than any with the Provincial. He considered war necessary if Hitler was to be stopped, and believed that there must be a whole-hearted support for the war effort in order to achieve victory as soon as possible. Before Christmas he was writing to ask which of the armed forces I would join. He himself was in the Observer Corps. David was in the Air Force, Bill was a cadet expecting to join it as soon as he finished school, Tom looked forward to joining the Army in due course. All our contemporaries in the village were in the Forces, mostly in the Army; the exception was my close friend Willie Fraser, also a Catholic and a conscientious objector. I wrote home very carefully, attempting to explain why I intended to remain where I was until compelled to leave. Dad shared the Provincial's opinion, though not for precisely the same reasons. When the Nazi forces swept across France my position became utterly incomprehensible, except in terms of cowardice. With so many lads from our area dead, or prisoners of war, I was simply a disgrace to my family and to the community; in my father's words, 'hiding in a monastery'. Once again he broke off relations, feeling bitterly the disgrace of having me as his eldest son. He had no doubt that I was regarded by many as evidence of his failure as a parent. 'Bring up a child in the way he should go, and when he is old he will not depart from it,' was still an accepted maxim in the Highlands in those days. He had been disgraced among Protestants by my religious deviance; this new deviance disgraced him everywhere. People were sorry for him and showed it by not mentioning my name.

The war did not disturb life at Woodchester in any great degree during that first year. We helped a short-handed local farmer to take in his hay; and were involved slightly one day in setting up a temporary reception for evacuees from a town on the Channel. The full tonsure was abolished and novices grew their hair again, after Vivian and I, walking briskly through a sleepy valley eight miles from the priory, were taken for German paratroopers. German aeroplanes appeared occasionally, and there was a warning against going out to watch 'dog-fights' in the sky. The priory was only six miles from the important air-base of Aston Down, whose turf-covered hangars the Luftwaffe with tireless mendacity claimed to have destroyed on several occasions. An incendiary bomb did land one night on a small mattress factory in the valley, and was dealt with speedily. There was no heavy bombing; the Luftwaffe was probing, not much more. When air-raid sirens went, it was suggested we should take shelter in the church crypt, a shelter of doubtful value in some minds. On the first night of alarm, I lay in bed listening to the characteristic sound of German aeroplanes, and a few distant explosions, and debating whether or not to go down to the crypt. Concluding that there was little point in doing so, I said some prayers and went back to sleep.

As the community produced nearly all its own fruit, vegetables, and eggs—and ate so little meat—there was no scarcity of food, except from the point of view of the novices, who would have groaned in any case under the community's normal regime. In the autumn we ate quantities of fruit surreptitiously while working in the garden, especially when picking pears and apples. In the winter our smuggled tea was accompanied sometimes by slices of 'stodge' (steam pudding), left over from the midday meal. There was seldom much left, as it was cutomary to offer second helpings at meals if there was enough, and lay brothers and novices were served first in the refectory always, by ancient custom. We stuffed ourselves as much as possible at midday in preparation for the long afternoons, especially during the bitter winter when the heating had broken down and the only fire in the noviciate quarters was a small smokey one in the common room. On some days it smoked so heavily that we preferred to huddle in our cells, heavily clothed, rather than be kippered with smoking eyes in the common room. For some of us, when weeks of ice and snow came to the Cotswolds, it was a relief to get out and walk among the loaded trees whose ice-coated branches grated weirdly if there was any wind and broke off frequently under the weight of frozen snow.

Surprisingly, it did not feel so cold in church. The Woodchester choir is very small, separated by a rood-screen from the nave. The screen was curtained, as were the windows, in accordance with wartime's blackout regulations. We wore heavy woollen knee-length stockings, and over our white ankle-length serve tunics and hoods even heavier black cloaks and hoods, until Easter. There was some heating in the church at weekends, and so we did not too badly, between that and our own human heat carefully conserved under heavy woollen material. We were not too cold to pray.

That was as well, since so much of the day was taken up with prayer, nearly five hours in all. It was important to get physical conditions right for prayer. More than one religious writer stressed that point, notably the medieval English mystic Richard Rolle. It was not necessary to kneel in order to pray, although kneeling during meditation was recommended to us at Woodchester, and sitting was not encouraged. Rolle considered it reasonable to sit; if the body was at ease and relaxed meditation would benefit. So, when done in my cell, I sat to meditate, as a rule. In choir we knelt, and discovered that there was an art in kneeling. Our tendency as beginners was to lean forward, arms over the desk in front of us, bottoms wedged against the seat behind. That posture, it turned out, was almost certain to result in the unpleasant swelling known as 'Housemaid's Knee'. To avoid that ailment it was necessary to kneel upright, back straight, weight bearing down directly on the knee and not pushed forward on the edge of the kneecap. At first it was difficult to maintain such a position, especially in the early morning, struggling against sleep and longing to put one's head down on the desk and doze. It was easier to meditate during the morning half-hour in the garden, walking slowly up and down one of the paths, in air made pleasant by seasoned smells and by the sound of birds. 'God Almighty first planted a garden,' said Francis Bacon, thinking of Eden. A garden, like a wood or forest, is by nature a holy place, a temple in which our awareness of God may be heightened if we move there quietly attentive to His presence. The Woodchester garden was precious at any time; not only when blossom was heavy in early Summer, or when roses or dahlias made a riot of colour beside the entrance path, but when wet box-hedges or potato shaws, or fallen leaves dominated the paths with their smell. It was clear rapidly that if the first thing to do, when undertaking meditation, was to compose oneself physically, then for me nothing could be better than steady pacing along a level path.

Gradually, however, other positions became more satisfactory. Sitting or kneeling three points were important: one's back should remain upright, hands should be joined lightly, breathing should be slow and steady. We did not know the word *mantra* then, but use of a *mantra* was invaluable in meditation; a simple word of phrase, expressing love, adoration, contrition, or faith, by repetition holding the spirit attentive to God's presence at the centre of one's own being. 'God have mercy, on me a sinner;' 'I love Thee, Jesus, my love above all things;' 'Glory be to the Father, and to the Son, and to the Holy Spirit.' There was an endless choice of phrases from popular devotion, from breviary and missal, from the Bible. Richard Rolle and Henry Suso suggested use of the name of Jesus by itself, and this practice developed later as a result of reading the story of a Russian pilgrim. By repeating the Holy name slowly, in time with heartbeat or a slow breathing rhythm, it was possible to slip quickly into meditation, or what Father Ferdinand Valentine called 'mental prayer', reserving the term 'meditation' for prayerful reflection on some religious theme or text.

The prayer of the presence of God, with which I had been vaguely familiar as a child, became increasingly significant. It linked easily with use of *mantras* and with various small pious observances recommended to novices, such as inclination of the head before the crucifix when entering or leaving one's cell, or making the sign of the cross at the beginning and end of some action, for example reading, or letter writing, or chopping wood.

A relatively new experience in prayer was the amount of bodily movement associated with the daily round of community prayer in choir. Any one of the 'hours' into which the Divine Office was divided, was prefaced by short preparatory prayer, mainly an act of adoration of the Blessed Sacrament, said kneeling. Everyone then stood up and made the sign of the cross, facing the altar; next turned around, faced inward across the choir, and recited *Gloria Patri et Filio, et Spiritui Sancto* ('Glory be to the Father, and to the Son, and to the Holy Spirit') while making a profound inclination. There were several degrees of inclination. The smallest inclination was simply a bending forward of the head, made at any mention of the names of Jesus or Mary. The 'slight' inclination was at an angle of approximately forty-five degrees from the waist and was made as the *Gloria* was recited at the end of each psalm or canticle, and at various other times. The 'profound' inclination was at an angle of 90 degrees or more; the body bending, in theory, until elbows rested on knees, which obviously was anatomically impossible for some people. During the psalms the brethren on one side of the choir stood, those on the other side not, alternately. So there was considerable movement while words were recited or sung; the whole action measured, rhythmical, and peaceful in its total effect. It was common to enter choir weary at nine o'clock, and to come out forty-five minutes later feeling wonderfully refreshed. We studied the psalms, in order to understand better what was being chanted, but it was not necessary to dwell analytically on each verse. There were various ways of responding to the psalms. One was to pick out a verse, or phrase, or even one word in a psalm, reflecting on it while reciting the rest; another was to enter into the mood of a particular psalm, contrite or grateful or rejoicing; yet another was to let the whole action become a great *mantra* whose steady beat first released mental and physical tension and then helped the soul to rest in awareness of God. The experience of sung Vespers on Sunday was a weekly high point, given that the community was singing fairly competently.

A high point in each day was Compline, followed by the singing of *Salve Regina* in a double-line leisurely procession out of choir and though the rood screen into the nave. All processions in Woodchester were leisurely and peaceful. On Rogation Days we drifted slowly round the garden, in early morning, singing litanies and sprinkling young dew-laden crops with blessing and holy water. Every Sunday in May there was a procession from the church through the garden and down the road back into the church, in honour of Our Lady. The Rosary was recited and Marian hymns were sung happily in a slow, drowsy time which had resisted for nearly a century any attempts to alter it. The Woodchester parish was in essence a product of the romantic side of the Catholic revival, of Father F. W. Faber rather than of John Henry Newman, but with touches of devotion from the earlier period of Challoner's *Garden of the Soul*. The pace was set by the women of the parish, strolling along gently, eyes wandering over plum blossom, cabbages or roses, with equal amicability. 'Daily, daily, sing to Mary' or 'Hail, Queen of Heaven, the ocean star, Guide of the wanderer here below,' dragged out in time with the slow movement of elderly feet. The great procession was on the feast of Corpus Christi, when the Blessed Sacrament was carried by the Prior, walking under a silken canopy supported by four men, the brethren following two by two, the priests in bright vestments, and behind them the Children of Mary in blue and white, the schoolchildren in their smartest clothes, and then the main body of parishioners. The flower girls in white dresses and veils went ahead, walking backwards as they strewed the path with flower petals, from baskets which were refilled speedily by a group of intent small girls, solemn under their proud title of 'Fill-baskets'.

There was a wonderful feeling of peace about these Woodchester processions. Nobody was anxious; all our senses were involved gently; church and nature around us were united in one simple, relaxed act of worship. There was a similar peace indoors on Thursday and Sunday evenings when the service of Benediction was held; lighted candles clustered on the high altar, music, incense, bells; the Host raised in the monstrance; adoration and blessing, voices from the dimmed benches in the nave joining the community in cadences of prayer. Much was open to humorous comment, or witty criticism, but it was good to be there and to share in the unsophisticated, popular worship.

Holy Week and Easter came as the high point of experience of worship. There were still enough young, musically competent priests in the community to make full celebration of the Holy Week liturgy possible. I had never experienced *Tenebrae* before in any form: now nothing could be more moving than the tragic, piercingly beautiful litany which concluded *Tenebrae*, sung according to the Dominican rite on three successive nights. *Christus factus est obediens*, two cantors sang, and two replied *usque ad mortem* as the last light went out, and in the darkness we heard the slow, high, terrible words *mortem autem crucis*, and one great crash before kneeling down silently in the blackness. On the night of the Holy Thursday the community kept vigil, two at a time kneeling for an hour in the Chapel of Repose, with its massed candles and banks of heavy scented lilies round the tabernacle, where the Eucharist rested in preparation for Good Friday. Adrian and I watched between three and four o'clock in the morning, and it seemed a very short time after returning to bed before we were wakened again. Good Friday was indeed a day of mourning. There was no *Gloria* at the end of psalms, and everything was recited or sung in a subdued voice. Solemn silence was the rule all day, and the black cloak and hood were worn all the time, everywhere. The 'black fast' was observed: which meant that for breakfast there was two ounces of dry bread and a bowl of black, unsweetened coffee; for the main meal there was unlimited bread and a bowl of soup; supper consisted of dry bread and tea. We made the Stations of the Cross and sang the Passion according to St Luke in a full church at three o'clock in the afternoon. After *Tenebrae* that night bed was even more welcome than after crossing the Lairig Ghru in rain. I felt that I had never begun to appreciate the suffering of Christ, even faintly, before that Good Friday.

Saturday by contrast was a lightsome day of sweeping and scrubbing in preparation for Easter Sunday and the blessing of the house, when every room and passage would be sprinkled with holy water; and bread and lamb be blessed in the kitchen while we all sang cheerfully in the cloister, at the foot of the stairs, in Latin: 'I saw water issuing from the right side of the Temple, alleluia; and all to whom that water came were saved, and they shall say, Alleluia, Alleluia. Give thanks to the Lord; the Lord is gracious, his mercy endures for ever.' The joy of the risen Lord touched everyone that day, helped by kindly weather.

Father Anthony wrote this narrative during his last months as Rector of the University of Edinburgh to which the students and staff had elected him in 1979: his term ended in 1982. He expected then to have the leisure to complete this volume, but he was only able to revise it and extend it to its present point when he was elected by the British Dominicans as their Provincial, and thereafter he had no time to return even to conclude the sequence which breaks off here. When Provincial, he was paralysed by a series of strokes and had to learn once more to speak and write. Having done so, he has made minor technical changes in this book, but no substantial ones. If he had been able to complete the passage in which the text now ends, he would have spoken of the magnificent High Mass which was celebrated at Woodchester on Easter Sunday 1940. He himself was thrown into ecstasy by being asked to assist as pro-sub-deacon. He remarks today that his exaltation had its effect the next day when he fainted and was excused Matins and early rising for a fortnight, with a diet of bacon and eggs prescribed by his novice-master.

He was ordained priest five years later, at Blackfriars, Oxford, on 29 September 1945.